AF481289

About
SPIRITUAL ENERGY
YOUR GUIDE to
PERPETUAL JOY

WALTER E. BROACH, MLS, M.Msc., D.Msc

Revised and Expanded Edition

ISBN: 979-8-9899508-0-5   PaperBack
ISBN: 979-8-89021-493-5   eBook
ISBN: 979-8-89021-494-2   HardBack

Library of Congress Control Number:

With thanks to Ellen Weaver Broach, my fantastic
and brilliant editor and partner in this wonderful
work of spiritual truth.

TABLE OF CONTENTS

Foreword	**xi**
CHAPTER 1 LIFE IN THIS WONDERFUL UNIVERSE	1
CHAPTER 2 YOU ARE A MICROCOSM OF THE MACROCOSM	11
CHAPTER 3 WHO YOU REALLY ARE	23
CHAPTER 4 THE LAW OF MOVEMENT AND CHANGE	33
CHAPTER 5 THE LANGUAGE OF THE UNIVERSE	44
CHAPTER 6 ENERGY THIEVES AND PSYCHIC VAMPIRES	55
CHAPTER 7 EXPRESS YOUR TRUE SPIRITUAL SELF	65
CHAPTER 8 THE MYSTICAL MAGIC OF MIND	75
CHAPTER 9 PURPOSE IN LIFE	85
CHAPTER 10 THE ROAD TO HAPPINESS	93
CHAPTER 11 THE OTHER SIDE	103
CHAPTER 12 THE SPIRITUAL PATH TO NIRVANA	112
CHAPTER 13 PREPARE FOR YOUR SPIRITUAL FUTURE	119
CHAPTER 14 GO FORTH WITH JOY	131
About the Author	137

FOREWORD

You are a spiritual entity or a soul walking around in a physical body. Most people have this truth exactly backward, believing that we are biological creatures either with or without that nebulous thing called a soul. *About Spiritual Energy* gives extensive information few people understand or have ever heard about the relationship between body and soul. This includes such elemental information as what your soul is, where it is located, how you communicate with it, and when you and your soul become one.

This book combines metaphysical ideas and actual science with practical suggestions on developing spiritual strength in your life. It provides you with an in-depth introduction to the subject. It gives specific ideas for spiritual self-development that can lead you to a life of happiness, prosperity, and self-esteem. This book contains metaphysical information that can prepare you for your existence not only in this life, but your life after your soul departs from your body. We know this time as death, but what dies? The entire universe consists of energy. The first chapter explains how death is just a term invented to describe the time when our bodies stop functioning and cannot survive as tenable human beings while still existing on earth.

People often think the word *spiritual* has something to do with religion. That can be true, but religion is often the antithesis of spirituality. People organize religions to make rules for people to follow to go to heaven, nirvana, or wherever. They give specific guidelines which a person must obey if they want to get to the promised land and they advertise the entity labeled God or god as being in control of all things. Spirit is the invisible energy that permeates the universe. It is everywhere and is an intimate part of your every thought, action, feeling, and experience. Humans form religions to control humans. Spirituality accepts the idea that spiritual energy is always with us and experiences everything we do. It is not more intelligent than us, nor is it subservient to us.

From what we have learned from science in the past few hundred years, it should be obvious that we do not die. And no, this truth does not have to challenge any religious beliefs or ideologies you may have. It is merely the truth. Look! You are composed of energy. Strictly defined, energy is the capacity or power to do work, such as the capacity to move an object in a direction by applying force. It can exist in various forms, such as electrical, mechanical, chemical, thermal, or nuclear. You can transform it from one state to another. Your body, your thoughts, your memories, and everything in the universe is energy. Your soul is energy.

People say God is everywhere. Is energy God? Is this fundamental energy what we call the ether God? People describe their soul as a *life force*, a power that connects living entities with interactions that scientifically recognized parties cannot explain. The primary energy in our lives is electromagnetic. It manages such things as running our computers, sending a picture from the transmitter to our televisions, and the power needed to run our physical bodies. You can call it whatever you want, but it is still energy. For this book, we will call it spiritual energy, and we will explain how it can help you improve your life in myriads of ways. Spiritual energy is the universal life force that runs through everything. It manifests as animals, plants, humans, stars, mountains, lakes, space, you, and everything in the universe. It is the be-all of everything, and it runs through everything.

People often refuse to admit that there is such a thing as spiritual energy. A few scientists recognize the fact, but most of them look out into space, where they can't see anything, and call it *dark matter* or *dark energy.* They may call it whatever they want, but it is spiritual energy. Ancient people called it *ether, quintessence, divine,* and other things. People will say that there is a difference between all those forms of energy, but the fact still is, they are all composed of raw energy, which is invisible or spiritual energy. It is wise of you to recognize your spiritual energy. When you accept its reality and cooperate with it, you can improve your mental, physical, emotional, and spiritual existence while on earth.

About Spiritual Energy will particularly interest those who have experienced trauma in their lives, those who have questions about their religious faith, and those who accept the fact that they are spiritual beings. It will help you develop a clear focus on your spirituality and help you understand how you can use your spiritual essence to help you develop inner strength, happiness, and the ability to overcome obstacles that interfere with your success in life. Best of all, it is about a fascinating subject.

CHAPTER 1

LIFE IN THIS WONDERFUL UNIVERSE

If you are old enough and intelligent enough to read this page, you were alive a few months ago and will keep living in the physical reality for at least a few more years. And believe it or not, you will still be alive one thousand years from now, two thousand years from now, and forever. Your body may cease functioning, whither, and disappear, but the energy from which it formed will still be viable. The energy keeps on vibrating and changing.

The time you spend on earth is a beautiful time for you to prepare for your spiritual existence when your time on earth ends. Many people believe that when our time on earth ends, it is the end of our existence. People can believe anything they want to believe, and they have every right to do so. Even those who refuse to accept the idea of spiritual energy, souls, and various forms of spiritual life can decide for themselves what they believe. They can also choose to be happy, filled with joy, or even be unhappy during their time on earth. The vast majority of us would desire to experience a feeling of inner joy. Our time on earth is a fantastic opportunity to gain experience on how to develop happiness, inner joy, and wisdom to carry with us when we transition into a more spiritual existence.

In the early days, people worried more about survival than whether they were dead or alive. When someone's body stopped moving and smelled, they figured it would not help the group survive, so it wasn't necessary to keep the body around. They didn't think it was dead; they just thought it had lost the ability to help with the hunting or whatever it did when it was still moving. Someone eventually called the non-moving body *dead*. Since then, people have been working diligently to produce ways to define the terms *dead* and *alive*. The definitions of life and death continue to evolve to this day.

Here is an example of those definitions: *life is the quality that distinguishes the difference between functioning beings and a dead body.* That sounds good, but it defines nothing. Another definition of life is that *life is a quality that makes a difference in whether we are alive or dead.* Here is another one: *to be alive, an organism must have the ability to reproduce and grow.* People reproduce and grow, so while they do that, they are alive. That is intelligent reasoning. Please note that viruses, mold, infections, and particles like germs can reproduce and grow. Some bacteria live near deep-sea thermal vents that use hydrogen sulfide instead of oxygen to live. And please note that invisible matter or energy also can expand, reproduce, and grow.

Spiritual Energy Is Invisible Energy

Have you ever noticed that people, animals, and other living creatures such as fish and spiders are curious and like to move around and explore their environments? Everything changes, but is it from curiosity or some unnamed, natural phenomena? The vibratory actions of every particle cause movement, and the movement causes change. Change expresses itself just the same as curiosity does. It appears always to be seeking something or attempting to express itself somehow. Every tiny particle of spiritual energy has this same tendency. It often becomes subdued in human beings who crimp their own curiosity because of the stresses of youth. They learn to be quiet around adults; teachers in school won't allow them to ask questions; they hear things like "little girls and boys are to be seen and not heard." Curiosity is a trait of all energy, whether or not it looks like it's moving. This curiosity trait is one of the significant factors that make life on earth so rewarding.

Each particle of energy is continuously vibrating, moving, and changing. It is natural for it to vibrate and change. It strives for the harmony it develops with other energy while existing in a physical body, just as it does while in its spiritual state. Incredibly, there is more cooperation, balance, communication, and pure love in the fifty to eighty trillion spiritual particles of energy in our bodies than in the measly seven or eight billion people living on earth. Each spiritual particle also has a memory.

Along with memory, it has the power of thought. People often believe that disembodied spirits have a great deal of wisdom or can heal diseases we cannot heal while running around on earth. Let's be honest about this. You are composed of the same material that is filling up the rest of the universe. Why should the spiritual energy outside you be any smarter than the spiritual energy inside you? It is the same energy, only in different forms. Even doctors admit they can do all the work possible and feed the body all kinds of drugs, but it is the body that inevitably heals itself. They will also say they always have better results with a patient who has a cheerful outlook than with someone with a negative attitude. That is the work of our spiritual essence acting under its current emotional feeling.

The definition of dead is *deprived of life, lacking the power to move, feel, or respond.* This is a good definition, but it misses the truth by a mile. Supposedly dead bodies still have life in them, no matter what materials go into building them. The spiritual energy which energizes them can feel, move, and continuously respond to their environment. The universe's fundamental particles, such as quarks, electrons, bosons, and atoms, which are invisible to the eye, continuously merge, grow, expand, and vibrate. Everything is energy. Here's a straightforward definition of living: *to be alive, an organism must have the ability to breathe.* That is a clear, concise explanation. But there is a parasitic blob known as Henneguya salminicola that does not breathe and is alive. It has no respiratory genes. It spends its whole life infecting the dense muscle tissues of fish and underwater worms.

Over time, people distinguished between energy one can see and energy one cannot see as physical energy and invisible or spiritual energy. But there is a kicker in that people today discount the idea of spiritual energy. They just call all invisible but active energy, *energy.* Once people believed that to be living, an organism must be able to respond to, interact with, or adapt to the environment in which it exists. Someone supplemented the definition by stating that a living entity should possess top organization and the capability to get nutrients, store energy, and use energy to meet its desires or necessities. It is also said that a living creature must have the ability to maintain internal stability under any stimulation or situation that would disrupt its normal function or condition. It must be able to expand, grow, or experience change while surviving in its environment.

They did not realize that they were describing everything in the universe, and none of these definitions fully explain what it is to be alive. To this day, even our most outstanding and most well-known scientists and researchers have failed to come up with a universally accepted definition of what life is.

Energy Lives

The next bit of information is deep, but is essential for a clear understanding of how universal energy works. Albert Einstein developed the theory $E = mc2$. His formula tells us that energy equals matter, and matter and energy are the same. The universe is a massive living creature of energy. If energy is matter, then you are a walking, talking entity of energy. Your spiritual essence is you, plus all the energy you continuously receive and disperse. The primary energy of the universe forms into fields that create ripples from which tiny particles evolve. Every particle of energy is a ripple in an electron field, and every particle of light is a ripple in a photon field. Particles such as quarks, muons, and neutrinos combine with the Higgs field to become the building blocks of matter. The Higgs field is a field of energy existing in every region of the universe accompanied by a fundamental particle known as the Higgs boson, which continuously interacts with other particles, such as electrons. Particles that interact with this field are "given" mass like how an object passes through molasses and becomes larger and slower as it passes through it.

These living building blocks are much like human stem cells. These are the materials that develop into every conceivable type of matter found throughout the universe. Each particle expresses energy and is invisible to the naked eye. We can't see them, and they are active everywhere. A quark can speed through your brain right now. You do not feel the quark because it has no mass. Being invisible and often without matter, these particles are incorporeal. Being incorporeal means they are nonmaterial, nonphysical, ethereal, and, as many would say, spiritual. They are spiritual forms of energy. These particles often move into other fields like the Higgs field. One particle called the Higgs boson, often called the God particle, meets with other particles to form new materials and new particles. These new materials develop into new particles that bump into one another or merge with myriads of other particles, forming different new materials.

Some of these new particles are spiritual and some physical. These new materials include the essential ingredients that build everything physical in the universe. They are like stem cells in the human body that can develop into trillions of bodily cells.

It is difficult for many people to grasp the idea that everything in the universe is alive, but the fact that all energy is living forces one to think about and even question the concept of life and death. Since our body is composed of energy and energy is indestructible, although our physical body will someday be gone, our energy will still exist. Most people call the invisible life in our bodies the *soul.* If we want to achieve happiness and joy in our future, it is a good idea for us to do something about it right now.

Albert Einstein said, "Everything in the universe is vibration." No one has ever proven him wrong on this fascinating piece of information. Anything that can move, grow, and reproduce is alive. Every speck of energy in the universe has the power to move. Each cell can reproduce by joining with another cell. Every bit of energy can grow by combining with another speck of energy. That means that every particle and cell that exists in the universe is living. You are a collection of billions and trillions of these tiny particles. Before you arrived here on earth, every atom, molecule, and cell in your body was living. All energy is alive. What we call dark matter is alive. Dark energy lives and all so-called invisible energy is alive no matter where it is and at what time it exists. Wherever any aspect of energy is, it is vibrating and alive. You may look at a supposedly dead body, a rock, or a mountain and believe they are only dead matter. That is easy to think because, to our eyesight, they are not moving. The idea of deadness goes back to the earliest definitions of life: *If it moves, it lives. If it doesn't move, it's dead.* In the past, they did not have the scientific equipment that would enable them to discover that there is movement in everything, however slight. If everything in the universe moves, then the universe is living. There will continue to be arguments about what is alive and what is dead for a long, long time—until someone proves there is actually such a thing as *dead,* as compared to alive.

Our souls are infinite

Every cell in your body has been living since the dawn of time. Each particle of energy has all the elements it needs to live. Every particle can adhere to other particles. Every particle can sense other particles near it. Each particle can perceive sounds and information from anything with which it comes into contact. Each particle influences and gets influenced by every other particle with which it comes into contact. Your body needs to have this communication between its different organs and cells to work efficiently. If you are working on a project with one or two other people, you must communicate with those other people to carry out your task. It is the same with your cells. That energy is conscious has been known to us for close to a hundred years. In 1940, Claude Elwood Shannon, the "father of the digital age," realized that Boolean algebra coincided perfectly with telephone switching circuits, and he defined one unit of information as a bit. About that time, another scientist, John Archibald Wheeler, who worked on the Manhattan Project and helped Einstein develop a unified theory of physics, proclaimed, "Everything is information." In 1989, he announced, "Everything, from particles to forces to the fabric of space-time itself … derives its function, its meaning, its very existence entirely … from… yes-or-no questions."

Dr. Melvin Vopson from the University of Portsmouth in the United Kingdom developed a hypothesis called the mass-energy-information equivalence. It says that "information is the fundamental building block of the universe, and it has mass." These scientific theories and principles can get confusing, so it all means that elemental energy—or, as we say, spiritual energy—can perform any function of the universe. It means our spiritual energy—our souls—not only are infinite but also have the power to hold knowledge, which is information.

Life Comes from Life

A human being forms when a seed combines with an egg. Both the seed and the egg were alive before they merged. Life does not spring from dead anything. The energy in the seed and egg contained memories, feelings, and the ability to receive and pass on information and nourishment from whatever environment in which it existed. Now you may ask if that means you have had previous physical lives. When you recognize that different cells may have lived in one or more individuals in earlier lives on planet Earth, they may have had earlier lives. Some people seem to remember portions of their past physical lives. In some countries, such as India, reincarnation is an accepted belief. Because you are continually taking on fresh energy and shedding old energy, any memories are likely to be partial and disorganized. After all, even in our present existence, we often forget childhood experiences, and even the experiences we think we remember may be false. Memories can be fallible.

We stop the heartbeat of animals before we eat them. Cows eat grass that is alive. They chew it down and receive nourishment from it. Most people do not realize that there are plants that eat other living creatures. The Venus flytrap is an insect-eating plant. The aquatic waterwheel plant (*Aldrovanda vesiculosa*) occupies the waters of almost every continent. It has spindly underwater flaps that quickly tighten around unsuspecting marine animals such as trumpet snails, mosquito larvae, and fish food, which it devours. The sundew plant primarily eats insects. Heck. When you get down to basics, human cannibals eat other people. Energy continuously consumes and creates changes in different energy sources.

Animals eat plants, and plants eat animals. Human beings consume both plants and animals. We take away a cow's ability to take part in its everyday activities and then cut it up to make steaks we cook in an oven or on a barbeque pit. We deprived the cow of the ability to breathe, and then we take it apart and cook it. It has been through a lot of difficulty and pain. But if it were dead, there would be no nourishment. You could not benefit from eating it. Life does not come from something that has no life. The once-active cow has gone through a great deal of change. The energy it had when it was up and physically alive is still generating. It just exists under different circumstances.

To continue to function as human beings, we need to breathe. We breathe air. Air is a mixture of gases along with a variable amount of water vapor. There would be no reason for us to breathe if we weren't taking nourishment from the air. If the ingredients in the air were not alive, we would get no nutrition from them. In fact, there are certain gases, such as carbon monoxide or even natural gas used for heating, which will quickly stop your human functionality if you breathe them rather than air. But these gases are also living because their ingredients continuously vibrate. Anything that vibrates is living, and all matter vibrates. As stated previously, early humanoids believed anything that moved was alive. Although there have been myriads of definitions of life and living, no explanation is better than saying everything that vibrates is living or alive. The universe is a massive organism of living energy.

You are a mass of vibrating energy

We need water to continue to function as viable beings. One molecule of water consists of H_2O. That is, one oxygen atom bonded to two hydrogen atoms. Oxygen atoms in water have a slightly negative charge, while hydrogen atoms are slightly positive. We can freeze water and turn it into ice or boil it and turn it into steam. Whatever we do with water, the hydrogen atoms and the oxygen atoms still vibrate, only at different rates. They are consistently moving and are alive. Every drink of water we ingest affects us. Water can help us feel better, or if we swallow too much of it, it can suffocate us and force us into another state of existence, which most people call death. But this state of existence is not one of death because every particle of matter or energy has existed since the dawn of time and will keep vibrating and existing until the end of time. Each particle of energy has all the attributes it needs to live. Each particle has the power to sense the particle next to it and exchange messages with it. This communication is continually going on.

It boils down to the fact that the universe is composed of energy—visible energy and invisible energy, which certain people call spiritual energy, although all energy is spiritual energy. People have many terms for it. Many people do not believe there is anything spiritual. They admit energy can be invisible. That is why this type of energy is called invisible energy. Countless people define radio waves, electricity, sunshine, radar waves, and other energy sources as invisible energies. Many people accept the fact that all energy is spiritual. We can believe anything we want to believe.

Dr. Stuart Hameroff, a physicist, and Sir Roger Penrose, a mathematical physicist at Oxford University, developed a consciousness theory. They claim that "we maintain the soul in microtubules of the brain cells."

When we enter the phase known as clinical death, the information in our brain still exists and returns to the universe while still living. That agrees with this book's thesis, which maintains that there is no such thing as death, only changing energy forms. Spiritual energy is universal. In fact, you are a microcosm of the universe. You might call yourself a universe, considering that you are an individual entity composed of many functioning energy types. The macro universe has stars, planets, moons, and all kinds of objects circulating throughout. Blood vessels, bones, organs, and all sorts of small matter are continuously engaged in keeping your body functional. You are a mass of vibrating energy, and you are a spiritual soul using a physical body to function while you are on earth. You are a microcosm of the macrocosm.

THOUGHTS

- People believe whatever they want to believe
- We do what rewards us
- During "clinical death, " the information in our brains still exists
- Our soul separates from our body at so-called death
- The universe is totally composed of energy
- We experience many situations throughout eternity
- Life comes from life
- The universe is a colossal thought or knowledge field
- You determine your future

CHAPTER 2

YOU ARE A MICROCOSM OF THE MACROCOSM

As human beings, we think of ourselves as unique forms of life. We believe we are superior creatures to all the animals in the world. We think we are unique. But we are only one type of expression of the universal whole. Our spiritual essence, formed from the universe's base material, comes together in human form. Throughout the universe, there are many other forms of life. In fact, there is life in every speck of material in the visible and invisible areas of the universe. There are stars, planets, solar systems, and many other kinds of living entities. They are all formed from the raw spiritual energy of the universe. We as humans are an accumulation of trillions and trillions of separate parts working together in supposed unity and harmony. But in many disabled or diseased individuals, all aspects of their bodies do not move and act together. It is just like the earth, which has continual weather-changing patterns. Yes, it is one planet, but it comprises many individual people, rivers, lakes, islands, mountains, cities, states, pieces of dirt, and spiritual energy. There is some activity type on all planets, stars, and every other object that lives in the universe.

You are a microcosm of the macrocosm. You are a miniature replica of the universe. You are composed of the same ingredients as the universe during your physical life, and you go through similar changes as the universe. You are a universe of your own. This idea is challenging for many people to accept or understand. It is difficult for many to look at a tree and believe it is a living being, even though we plant them and expect them to grow. The tree grows, communicates with other trees and plants, and responds to the treatment it receives from humankind. It also responds to the climate and the environment in which it gets planted. Mountains grow and recede, oceans rise and shrink, flowers blossom and sleep during cold weather, and continual change throughout the universe is eternal. Humankind just is one living entity among trillions and trillions of other living entities. Humankind is also fortunate because the combination and distribution of its spiritual energy allows it to experience many positive and negative circumstances during its earthly existence. While our spiritual energy, which is the totality of each of us, exists in human form, our physical feelings are more substantial than our feelings while in the purely spiritual state. We are better able to improve our feelings of joy, love, anger, pity, guilt, and every unique feeling we may have. The feelings you experience give the time you spend on earth a fantastic amount of importance in your travel through eternity.

You and Your Soul Are One

From the moment of your conception, your soul forms and develops along with your physical body. The totality of your physical and spiritual or invisible energy is your soul. Your soul, in this present lifetime, emerges from the spiritual essence of both parents. This energy passed down from one or both of our parents could have been your energy from a past life, which explains why people have feelings that they have been reincarnated. People have historically talked about their souls as if they are some cloudlike things floating around their insides. I remember seeing a movie when I was a child where the hero died, and a small, round cloud flowed from his stomach area toward the heavens, where it eventually disappeared. It was supposed to be his soul leaving his body on its way to heaven. Your soul is composed of your entire being. It is all the energy that enables your body and mind to do what it deems necessary to accomplish its goals and needs. You are a walking, talking soul that has developed a physical body that helps you to operate successfully as a human being.

Hold your hand about one-half inch to three or four inches away from your arm and drift it back and forth. You can feel the energy radiating from your body. What you will feel is spiritual energy. It is the outermost part of your soul. If you've never felt the energy radiating from your body, you may have to move your hand closer. It is easy to do, and most people can see this energy. It looks like heat radiating off of the highway when you drive through the desert on a hot summer day. To see your aura, you can hold your hand out in front of you with your fingers spread out. Then focus your eyes on your fingertips or look just past them. If you don't see your aura immediately, allow your eyes to glaze a bit, and you should be able to see it. Most small children can easily see auras, but they do not even notice them when they are adults.

Your skin glows in the dark. A few years ago, Japanese scientists used ultrasensitive cameras to prove that human bodies emanate a glow like fireflies. We can see this glow best late in the afternoon and is faintest late at night. This glow radiates mostly from the forehead, cheeks, and neck. It is part of your aura. Many people believe they can't see them. Some people do not think we have auras and will never see them, no matter how hard they try. They will believe whatever they want to believe and always do their best to prove what they believe is right.

Before you are born, you take on trillions of physical and spiritual or invisible cells attached to you from your parents' cells. You immediately start taking on nourishment and some of the energy your mother is receiving from the air she breathes, the liquid she takes in, and the solid matter she consumes. You also hear noises and conversations from your mother and others who are close to you. During the nine months that you are developing to become a full-fledged baby, you are also taking in all your mother's thoughts, emotions, and any information with which she comes into contact. You hear the same words and noises she hears; you sense the smells she smells, and you continuously experience everything she experiences. When you first see the light of day, you are already experiencing a full range of emotions. Everyone has a default emotional range. As with all energy, both physical and spiritual, your feelings are in a continual state of change, although it may be a narrow range. One baby may be happy most of the time, while another baby might be whiny and unhappy most of the time. The average feeling expression of the child is the soul's default range of emotions. It is something that can be significantly improved or damaged during one's physical life on earth.

Your Energy Is the Same as That of the Universe

Your present physical life is a beautiful opportunity for you to adapt your emotional default level to one of love and happiness. It is also a time in which you can develop wisdom. Many people will experience sadness, anger, and possibly hate throughout their lives. Their spiritual energy will continue to keep these emotions when their bodies dissipate into spiritual energy at the end of their physical lives. While these traits develop in your physical body, they also grow in your spiritual body. These emotions and feelings also cruise throughout the larger universe.

Your everyday experiences replicate the activity of the energy throughout the universe. Right here on earth, we have tornados, earthquakes, hurricanes, blizzards, and all kinds of disruptive weather phenomena. The same type of weather activity happens on other planets and stars throughout the cosmos. Astronomers have discovered massive storms of all types on the different planets and stars in our heavens. We also have storms in our bodies, such as when we have an upset stomach or when our appendix acts up, and a doctor removes it. Many people have heart disease, diabetes, cancer, and high blood pressure. These diseases do not differ from the disruptions that occur throughout the rest of the universe, only in other forms and under various labels.

During your existence on earth in human form, your physical parts are in continual communication with one another. When you eat, drink, breathe, or dispose of waste, your body parts are working harmoniously together, often without you knowing what is going on. This type of bodily activity continually goes on, causing changes that affect your body parts' health, weight, and usability. The same activity goes on in the macro universe. We rarely think about it, but the universe contains the same spiritual energy as we do that allows our energy-containing information to spread throughout the heavens. Our bodies are like a universe to our cells, just like we are cells to the totality of the universe. The universe contains us, and we hold our cells. We continuously take on spiritual energy from our surroundings every moment we experience physical life. We shed tiny morsels of our spiritual energy that drift off into the larger universe every moment.

Change Is a Basic Fact of Life

At your conception, your parents' combined energies formed a zygote that subdivided into smaller cells. These cells grew and became all the organs of your physical body. A baby's heart beats within six weeks of conception, and its pain receptors are present throughout its body by sixteen weeks after fertilization. Nerves link these pain receptors to the brain's thalamus and subcortical plate by twenty weeks, after which the unborn child can react to stimuli by recoiling. Babies are already beginning to feel the atmospheric energy in their mother's immediate surroundings. They will be affected happily if her surroundings are happy. They will be affected sadly if her surroundings are sad. Every infant's primary feeling is the beginning of a lifelong phenomenon of reacting to others' emotions while we are on earth. It is called change. Every particle of energy is always vibrating and either causing change to other particles or being changed by other particles.

People resist change in their lives. Think about how many people keep working at a job they detest because they believe they need the money to live. Think about those who just stay where they are because they think they cannot get another job or because they are just plain lazy. People remain in unhappy marriages because they cannot figure out a way to leave them. There is comfort in resisting change. It seems like the simple thing to do. But change happens anyway. Painful experiences keep getting unhappier until they force change, or someone dies, which is change.

Plato's allegory of the cave is a beautiful example of how people fear change. In it, there were a bunch of people chained to a wall in a dark cave for many years. One man somehow breaks free and leaves the cave. It is difficult for him to appreciate his freedom until he sees how beautiful the outside world is. When he realizes how incredible his freedom is, he returns to help the other people get out of the cave. They resist and don't believe him. Not one person will leave the cave. The people refusing to leave the cave is a perfect example of how people feel about change. It terrifies them. And think about it. If you improve your life even just a little, you will experience some change.

At birth, your organs communicate with one another just as you communicate with other people as an adult. The average 154-pound man has about seventy trillion cells in his body. To estimate the actual number of cells, a biologist team in 2016, led by Ron Milo from the Weizmann Institute of Science, reviewed all the literature on the microbe populations that live inside us. They found that a man between twenty and thirty years old, weighing about 154 pounds and 5 foot 7 inches tall, would have about thirty-eight trillion human cells in his body. When you add bacterial cells, the total is close to seventy trillion cells. Compare that to the less than ten billion people living on earth today. There is more cooperation between your supposedly unintelligent cells than far fewer supposedly intelligent people living on earth.

You Are a Separate Universe for Your Cells

Each cell comprises many millions of molecules that continuously send messages to the cell next to it while doing its essential work. Cells respond to one another because of chemical or electrical stimulation. They also react in a robotic way to movement. You can call the transfer of messages between cells anything you want, however invisible, and therefore, spiritual energy produces it. Your cells talk to one another in a spiritual language that you, as a physical creature, never hear or even need to hear. If your cells work together to keep your physical body active, they must somehow know how to act and react with one another. The transfer of information travels from one cell to the cell next to it and down the line. Again, this is a form of spiritual communication. The needed information is passed from one cell to the next cell just as you give information to a clerk in a store when you want to buy something.

Your cells are doing the work that they are supposed to be doing. Some cells work to develop new tissue, while others work to repair tissue damage or clean up debris or send other messages along a neural path throughout your body. Inside each cell's nucleus are two strands of twisted chemicals covered with over twenty thousand genes that provide the basic blueprints for living on earth. These tiny bits of energy offer both the strength and the ability for you to think, move, change, and communicate. You are the possessor of a thriving universe of spiritual creatures. When you no longer exist in the physical environment, you will take many of them with you to live in the spiritual plane.

Your body parts continually communicate with one another. Your stomach will communicate with your brain when it is hungry or full. When your knee hurts, it signals your mind to help it stop hurting. You feel love and joy and even anger throughout your body. Whatever feelings you experience, you inundate the cells of your spiritual essence with the same emotions. They carry the same feelings with them and infect other cells of spiritual energy. These same feelings can also infect other living people through the process of contagion. Whatever we do affects ourselves as a universe. When we become angry, it interferes with our thinking process. Anger raises a person's blood pressure, and the high blood pressure shuts off nourishing energy to the brain. Angry people do not make intelligent or wise decisions. When you see politicians yelling and accusing their opponents of dishonest trickery, lying, and cheating, they are likely doing the same things they are screaming about. When the criticized person remains calm, they are likely innocent because they know they are innocent. Being falsely accused may hurt their feelings. It may embarrass them, but honest people have no need or reason to get angry unless in self-defense. The screamers are the ones likely doing the dirt. They scream about the innocent person to divert the focus from themselves.

It is a human predisposition to believe that everyone else thinks and acts the same as they do. Believing everyone thinks alike is a fallacy. Even in small families, there can be a tremendous difference of opinion. Even among siblings, there are often differences in thinking. Look at your family and ask yourself if everyone always agrees on every situation that comes up. There is a ninety-nine percent chance that there are differences, if only because each of us has our own unique experiences in life. Many preachers who preach about hell and damnation can only find sin and perdition. You will often hear about a preacher exposed for doing the very things about which they preach. Also, many politicians get caught doing the exact thing they accuse their opponents of doing. When this happens, there is always a lesson for both the accuser and the accused. While you are on earth, every cell in your body adjusts how it reacts to every situation that it experiences. It will take this information with it throughout its next period of eternity.

Each part of the body we wear while on earth can think, grow, and shrink as it continues to vibrate. When you think about this, it makes sense and helps you understand your total being's true spirituality. Suppose your organs and other parts of your body did not communicate with one another. How would they be able to help you achieve anything while existing together? How could you wake up in the morning after a full night of sleep? How could you even live?

Where Your Attention Goes, Your Energy Flows

As you age, you experience many situations that affect your mental, physical, and emotional well-being. How you react to these situations has a powerful effect on your soul. When you emerge from physical living to spiritual living, you keep your feelings, intelligence, and emotions. It is easier to improve all aspects of your soul while you are in physical form than in a purely spiritual environment. The physical expressions you come into contact with transfer quicker and have a more substantial impact in the physical matter environment than in one that is purely spiritual.

Just like the larger universe, your body does not always act as you desire. When you become ill and would rather work or play instead of feeling bad, your body sometimes acts like a disobedient child who needs your attention. You can learn from the experience or repeat it over and over until you know whatever you need to learn from the experience. Every painful experience of your life presents you with an opportunity to learn something helpful. You will have similar opportunities until you learn the lesson you need to learn. There is an expression, "Where your attention goes, your energy flows." Many people get caught up in the cycle of going from one awful experience to another. They worry and fuss about their troubles, and by the time one goes away, another one comes along. When this happens, they have something to learn. The unhappy episodes will continue until the person knows whatever lesson they need to learn. To discover your lesson, you need to examine your inner wants and opportunities to better your life. Only you can do this, and you must seriously want to improve your life. It will not hold you back if you decide to learn how to experience and feel the emotion of joy. You are responsible for your actions, your feelings, your health, and your relationships. If you want happiness or feelings of self-worth, it is up to you to develop them. When you depend on others for your joy, you become their slave and give them control of your spiritual well-being. Also, when you become dependent on others for your feelings, you never develop the spiritual strength to help others who may be in need.

Matter is an illusion

We can understand and feel the emotions of others. During your life, you produce feelings of every sort. At every moment, you receive spiritual information as feelings. When you are young, your parents may persuade you to stay away from specific individuals, groups, or areas of the world. They do not want you to be exposed to bad influences. Whether or not you realize it, they are doing the right thing for you. Wherever you are, and whoever you are with, you are picking up spiritual energy. It is just like when you put a rotten apple in a barrel of good apples. The rot spreads from the rotten apple to the good ones it touches. The energy from the people you associate with has a powerful effect on your whole being. It can quickly spread right to you.

Trillions of neutrinos, sometimes called ghost particles, pass through your body every second. Your skin cells get replaced by new cells every two to three weeks. Your blood cells are replaced every three to five months. Your lung cells replace themselves every two or three weeks, and even your liver cells continually get replaced. You change. Your thoughts evolve and everything in your life changes. You continuously travel down a path to return to the spiritual state of existence, although with different energy and ideas.

What we perceive as our physical universe is not physical or even material. It is invisible and immaterial. Niels Bohr, a noted quantum physicist, once stated, "Everything we call real is made of things that cannot be regarded as real." During the last hundred years, scientists have been exploring the relationship between energy and matter. These studies proved that the material universe was not the be-all of living matter and that matter is nothing more than an illusion. They realized that everything in the universe is energy. Everything being energy means that you, as an individual soul or person, are composed of trillions of individual spiritual cells that, because of their grouping together with minimal spacing, give the impression of being solid matter. This is also true for every rock, planet, chair, and so-called piece of matter throughout the macro universe.

We are beings of vibrating energy. Each atom in our so-called physical body spins and vibrates in its unique fashion and radiates its unique signature. When you view an atom's composition with a microscope, you see a tiny, almost invisible tornado-like vortex with many infinitely smaller energy vortices called photons and quarks. These are what make up the structure of the atom. As you focus even closer on the atom, you will view absolutely nothing. You will see a physical void, as atoms have no physical structure. When you get down to the minor details of the human configuration, there is nothing. Human beings have no physical form when they are examined in such a manner to get to their basic structure. Atoms are composed of invisible spiritual energy and have no physical structure. We have no basic structure, and our atoms have no basic structure. You, just as all supposedly physical things, don't have any physical structure. This may be difficult to comprehend, but what it means is that you are a soul walking around with the appearance of being a solid physical being.

You Are A Spiritual Being

Richard Conn Henry, professor of physics and astronomy, said, "Get over it, and accept the inarguable conclusion. The universe is immaterial, mental, and spiritual." The immaterial, mental, and spiritual universe is the understanding we know through the study of quantum mechanics. Our everyday experiences seem to prove that our reality is physical and material. It appears that our world is made of concrete and sensible things and that we live in an objective and practical world. The revelation that the universe is not composed of physical parts but is a humongous composition of invisible and immaterial energy waves came from the minds of Albert Einstein, Max Planck, and many others. Their discoveries are powerful proof that we are spiritual creatures living in a spiritual universe. Our souls are an integral part of this combination.

Everything we do and everything we experience affects our souls. Studies have shown that operating from positive emotions and peace within oneself can lead to a compelling and pleasant experience for the person emitting those emotions. And it is easy to understand that people articulating hateful feelings can turn a fortunate occurrence into something not so enjoyable. Feelings are contagious, just like the flu. Just as we know that the universe, the world, and each of us are spiritual energy, we know that energy is indestructible and vibrates.

Vibration is movement. When there is enough movement in anything, whatever the energy it is associated with will experience some change. Just as our bodies continually change, our emotions often change, and everything in the universe changes. Change is the one phenomenon that is universal and constant. Examine your own life. You have changed a great deal since you were born. You are bigger, stronger, and more able to speak and understand what is happening around you. Businesses start-up, grow large, shrink, and discontinue. You are continually changing and becoming healthier, weaker, smarter, and not so smart. You may be happy today and sad tomorrow. Your soul experiences everything precisely as you do. That is how life works. Good things happen to you, and everything is lovely. Someone steals your money, and things seem not to be good. As you continue to change throughout your life, it sometimes becomes confusing as to who you are or what you are. You are a spiritual entity. You are one special, unique soul with your own identity.

THOUGHTS

- You are a microcosm of the macrocosm
- You are a walking, talking soul using a physical body
- The human body radiates a glow
- Human emotions are in a constant state of change
- The human body always communicates with its separate parts
- It is natural for people to resist change
- The average 154-pound man has thirty-nine trillion cells in his body
- The universe is not composed of physical parts
- Energy is indestructible and vibrates

CHAPTER 3

WHO YOU REALLY ARE

Each of us correctly identifies ourselves as human. We are composed of trillions and trillions of spiritual cells parading around as human beings. Recognition of our spiritual essence is essential for us to understand who and what we are. We are composed of many trillions of tiny, tiny cells, ten thousand times smaller than a human hair's circumference. These cells are so small that only the most powerful equipment can detect them. Each cell is composed of spiritual energy. Each cell has the power to move, and each cell is continuously vibrating and will continue to shake and vibrate throughout eternity. Each cell can feel, think, understand, communicate, experience, and recognize the atmosphere. I will explain this in more detail in chapter 5.

You don't notice blood flowing through your veins. It just does it. A mosquito crawls across your arm, and you don't notice it until it sinks its stinger into your skin. You may not see it when it stings you, but you will probably develop an itch where it stabbed you. Many processes are going on in our bodies that we do not realize are going on. Our organs continuously communicate with one another, and we do not even notice it. Also, their cells communicate with one another. Is it automatic that when we swallow our food, it goes into our stomach and gets digested? Is it because that is what stomachs do? We put food into our mouths and then consciously or unconsciously chew it. Then we use our tongue and other parts of our mouth to deliver it to our esophagus, which gives it to our stomachs, which digests it and sends it to our intestines. Our intestines then send nutrients to the rest of our body. We do not consciously follow these behaviors, but our body's various parts are continually working and communicating with one another to accomplish these maneuvers.

One of the most beautiful features of the human body is how coordinated everything is. All our organs and parts work together in perfect harmony to allow for physiological, cognitive, and behavioral functions. Scientists have investigated how the assorted and different parts of the body cooperate flawlessly. They have found that cells use sugar to communicate at the molecular level. In other words, they are speaking with one another. As said earlier, combined cells make up everything with mass or everything that we perceive as solid. They provide the structure for everything and are 100 percent of us in our human manifestations. Your cells are involved in all chemical, biological, and communication functions. They work together to maintain your physical processes and come in many forms, shapes, and sizes. Some are round, while others are cubed, long, starlike, flat, or even shapeless. The tiniest cells can be as small as one-millionth of a meter. Larger ones can measure ten to one hundred micrometers in width.

You will experience all emotions during eternity

You are a conglomeration of these tiny cells composed entirely of energy. Every moment of your life, you are ingesting more cells, and every moment of your life, cells are leaving you. Each of these cells has the power to feel love, happiness, joy, and pain. You, as a fully developed human being, are supposed to have intelligence. Where does this intelligence come from if it isn't in your cells? How do you feel love and emotion if your cells can't handle these same things? Whenever you have pain anywhere in your body, that body part sends you a message that it needs help. This message is passed along through your nerves and the cells in your nerves vibrating against one another. Their language isn't spoken words or writing or hand signals. It is through vibration and touch, just as when you feel great pain and pray or shout out to God, the Great Pumpkin, or whomever your cells are calling out to for help. And you often listen to them and do something to help lessen the pain. Your cells are communicating to your spiritual mass with the pain they are sending you. Even paralyzed people can feel pain in whatever part of their body they cannot use. They cannot use the feature, such as a leg, because the nerves connecting it to the mass have been severed or smashed and rendered useless, but they can still feel the pain. Also, people who have lost arms or legs often feel what is called phantom pain. The body part is now totally spiritual, but still communicates with you. This transfer of knowledge and feeling happens throughout the universe.

You are one unique part of this fantastic universe. You continually affect the universe, and it always affects you. You are a spiritual emanation that currently exists in human form. Many people say that we are souls wearing bodies while we are on earth. People often quote the Bible to prove this.

An example is in 2Cor 4:16 (New Living Translation), "That is why we never give up. Though our bodies are dying, our spirits renew every day." Most religions believe in souls and the idea that upon death, our souls, which are spiritual energy, will leave our bodies and go someplace. That is true. The concept of spiritual life has been with us forever, and people have the right to believe or disbelieve the idea. People have argued about this for millennia and will continue to do so forever. If you can recognize that invisible energy is spiritual, it is easy to accept the idea of spiritual energy. Spiritual energy is invisible energy. Invisible energy is spiritual energy. You are one spiritual being that is a very tiny part of a much larger spiritual being. The universe is simply a larger living spiritual entity with trillions and trillions of physical masses. As you are a part of this humongous spirit, you are composed of the same ingredients as every other human. You are neither better nor worse than anyone else. You will have many moments of happiness, sadness, nirvana, and pain throughout eternity. It is your responsibility to decide what you want to experience. If you put no thought into what you want to have, you will be subject to the feelings, emotions, and sensations brought to you by others.

Labels are only labels

Billions of years ago, the universe's energy formed matter by matching different minuscule particles of itself to make physical forms. At first, the energy started forming stars and planets and eventually rivers, lakes, streams, and finally, small beings. Some of these little beings grew into animals like lions, tigers, fish, elephants, and humans. This spiritual energy is the same energy you are composed of today. While in human form, we can experience many forms of pain and pleasure, to the degree that we do not in a purely spiritual state. Over the years, humankind has grown larger. We have developed vocal cords for speech and flexible fingers to handle objects. We have also created trillions of gadgets for work and play. Right now, you are enjoying or maybe disliking your time on earth. Earth life gives you the opportunity to experience joy differently than you do when you are in a purely spiritual state. Whether your interest is love or hate, you are still a conglomeration of the same spiritual energy that flows throughout the larger universe.

While you exist in your physical form, and soon after you emerge from your mother's womb, you receive a name. Someone gives you a label to identify you and distinguish you from other people. People will identify you with this label for the rest of your life. Most people keep this label, but the name may be added to or changed during a lifetime. If your name is John Doe, you may get married and take the last name of the person you marry. John Doe may become the husband of Mary Morris and take her last name, so he is now called John Morris, Mary Morris's husband. Or she could take John's last name, and Mary Morris would become Mary Doe. Labels for people help us know who someone is talking about when they are not right in front of us. A label is a classifying word or name describing a person or thing. It can be accurate, inaccurate, restrictive, or expansive. A label does not need to be accurate or even truthful. For example, say your so-called friend calls you stupid. Your so-called friend is giving you a label. If you are dumb, which you probably are not, since you are reading this book, it is a lie and a false brand. Labels are just tags. We use them to describe things, people, and processes. They have nothing to do with who you are.

While experiencing our physical life, we most likely receive many labels. Say John Doe goes to school during his teenage years and plays on a sports team. He might have more labels. He might be called a student, a school kid, a scholar, an athlete, or even a no-good, ill-behaved brat. People can call him anything they want. They do not describe or identify who John is. The labels we attach to others give us something to use to identify them. They are only descriptions we invent about them and have a minimal basis in the need for truth. What about when you were a child, and another child called you "a rotten, no-good twerp." As a child, you became insulted, developed hurt feelings, and went home and dwelled on your rage. But labels are only labels.

You are always speaking to yourself

You receive labels throughout your physical life. When you were a child, some people may have looked at you and said, "Oh my, what a beautiful child," or "What a cute little girl (or cute little boy)." As you grow older, people continue to say things about you that may be good or bad. He's a rotten jerk; she's ugly as sin; you are a no-good muffin digger. These are only labels and change many times throughout life. These descriptions mean only what the person saying them or thinking them wants them to signify at the moment.

There is a danger in being labeled by others. Your soul or subconscious spiritual mind may believe the person calling you names is telling the truth and cause you to act out the meaning of your label. If someone tells you that you are no good, rotten, or worthless enough times, you might believe it. If you are highly suggestible, you might act that way unless you have a healthy support system. Have you ever been told, "You're your own worst enemy?" If you hear that one enough, especially if you are highly suggestible, there is no telling what you might end up doing to yourself. Besides, the person telling you that you are no good is hearing themselves speak, and their spiritual mind likely believes that they are also not good. Dumping on people is a two-edged sword.

Labels do not correctly identify, describe, or mean anything about you. They represent only what the labeler wants them to mean. When people give others unkind labels, they usually get insulted and react unpleasantly. The label is meaningless, except for what the person expressing it wants it to mean. You can make your own definition for the term. An example is, "When the idiot calls me a jerk, he means I am wise and powerful." The person doing the vilifying also hears what they say. They listen to what they say clearer than you do, and their essence believes them, too. You are always the first person to hear every word you speak. Every word and thought you say is spiritually aimed directly at yourself.

People can label you anything they want, but you are still a spiritual being and an integral part of the cosmos. When people discontinue their lives on earth, their souls return to the universe. When the heart stops beating, the organs no longer function. The blood stops flowing, and the information in the brain disburses into the universe. Resuscitate the body, and this information can go back into the brain. The entire episode will go down as a near-death experience. Don't revitalize the body and the data can exist forever in your soul as it continues its journey through eternity. This postulation is only one of many explanations for what the soul is. It recognizes that the energy of which we all are composed is eternal.

You Play Many Roles During Your Time on Earth

During your time on earth, you will play many roles. A role is a socially recognized behavior pattern, usually determined by your special status in society. It is also a part played by an actor or the description of the activities you involve yourself in. Your roles are the activities you need to be involved in to bring you peace, happiness, and love. Or, if you prefer, your roles can bring you anger, hurt feelings, and misery.

Say you are the mother of three children. One role you play is that of being a mother. This does not mean you are an exemplary mother, a terrible mother, or any other kind of mother. You may spoil your children to death or scream at them at least twice a day. You are still playing your role as a mother, and it has nothing to do with who you are. It is one activity you involve yourself in as you spend your time on earth. We use the roles we play to improve our ability to love and be more in tune with our identity. However, some people play roles that push them away from the loving, joyful, and wise souls they are meant to be.

Say you are in college or high school, and you play football. Football is a sport, so your role is to play football, and you may be labeled as a football player or as a high schooler or a high school football player. You get these labels to describe the roles you play. Labels have nothing to do with who you are. They are just used to describe you in a comfortable, convenient manner. People will identify with you as they understand who you are. They may identify you by the label someone else like your parents gave you or by the name you give them. It is only how others recognize you. It may have nothing to do with who you are. You are one of trillions and trillions of spiritual souls existing throughout the universe. You are, in reality, a spiritual being. You are totally composed of spiritual energy. You can touch, feel, and see your body, but it is composed of spiritual energy structured so that you can see and feel it. You have a brain that is visible when you expose it. You also have a mind, which is composed of spiritual energy that you cannot see or feel because it is spiritual.

The scientific community has traditionally tried to define the mind as the product of brain activity. The brain is defined as the organ in the head exerting centralized control over the body's other organs. It is said to be the command center for the nervous system and the coordinating center of feeling and intellectual activity. One definition says it handles the exercise of thought and the control of speech. It may be responsible for the exercise of thought, and it may control our speech, but it does not explain where the thought comes from or what produces thought, or how we develop our thinking.

Your Mind Lives in Your Spiritual Essence

Supposedly, there are three sources of thought. It is said that thought results from sense perception activated by sense organs feeding the brain, which generates a thought to transmit to the mind. It is also believed that thought comes from the subconscious mind that stores conscious experiences. And finally, another belief is that thought comes from our soul that maintains hidden memories from our past life. Accepting the spiritual nature of the mind clears up the confusion of brain, thought, and mind ideas. The mind is a series of elements or processes in an individual that feels, perceives, thinks, wills, reasons, and judges. It is a mental process as opposed to physical activity. Being mental means it is invisible and spiritual, and your thoughts come from your soul or your spiritual essence.

One theory states that there is one absolute mind in the universe with which we are all connected. Another approach regards the mind as a universal property of matter, of which we all can tune in. Modern research tells us that the mind goes far beyond the physical mechanisms of the brain. It regulates the energy and information flow within each of us. It is said to be responsible for our thoughts and feelings, our expression of opinions, and interpreting perception, memory, emotion, imagination, reason, and unconscious cognitive processes. In simple language, it is our soul. It exists not only in our brains, but also throughout our physical body and the aura surrounding our body. We occasionally hear someone say they are a soul walking around in a body. They are telling the truth as the soul controls and regulates the body. How it does so is only now beginning to be understood because it is expressing its magic and power on the quantum level.

The brain is a multilayered ecosystem of organized neurons, circuits, networks, and brain areas. The neurons emit pulses called *spikes* that last about one millisecond. Each neuron fires (emits a spike) in the order of ten times per second. These neural spike signals circulate throughout the brain in complex flows that interact with other signal patterns and channels through extensive multilayered feedback loops and synchronized, oscillating firing patterns. Thinking is still poorly understood, but it involves interactions between signaling pathways that carry information about the world and neurons representing information in working (short term) memory. The neural circuits representing working memory do so via sustained firing until they are deactivated.

Decision-making appears to be a winner-takes-all process in which many neuron clusters representing alternate action choices compete by inhibiting one another. Evidence supporting each action choice increases the spiking activity of the neurons expressing that choice. These neurons inhibit the neurons representing other choices, leading to a multi-way competition among neuron clusters. Eventually, the evidence supporting one option as optimal overtakes all the others. It suppresses the alternatives, becoming the clear winner.

Once one hypothesis or choice overtakes others, the activated neuron cluster (called a cell assembly) produces action, such as announcing a decision or acting to achieve something. This description is a simplification of what occurs based on current theories and models. None of this is definitively determined yet. An easier way to put it is that your spiritual cells debate one another and have a vote. The majority wins — just like in an election.

The bottom line is that every human being is a manifestation of spiritual energy composed of the same material and innate qualities as every other human being. We hear that "sticks and stones may break my bones, but words can never hurt me." That is wrong. Words can hurt like the dickens. And when we give a person a cruel label or condemn them in any manner, we are possibly pushing their spiritual essence into experiencing unhappiness or pain. We also expose ourselves to unhappiness and pain when we treat others with disrespect. Our subconscious hears what we say and believes we are talking about ourselves.

We are spiritual creatures walking around in a physical body formed from spiritual energy. This energy is ever-changing and ever developing. It has feelings and communication abilities and is in a continual state of change. We can help ourselves by taking care of ourselves with love, respect, and tenderness. And when we learn to treat others as well as we treat ourselves, the environment we exist in can be one of supreme happiness. We need to direct those changes we go through positively.

THOUGHTS

- You are composed of trillions of spiritual cells
- Your organs constantly communicate with one another
- You are a spiritual entity wearing a body while on earth
- You have the same ingredients as all other humans
- You determine what you will experience on earth
- Earth life can be a time to learn about happiness and joy
- You will receive many labels while on earth
- You will play many roles while on earth
- Your mind lives in your spiritual essence

CHAPTER 4

THE LAW OF MOVEMENT AND CHANGE

John F Kennedy, past President of the United States, once said, "Change is the law of life." He was right. We know the universe is composed of vibrating energy. Anything that vibrates is moving. Anything that moves causes change. As the universe solely comprises spiritual or invisible vibrating life, it is eternally experiencing change. And every place in the universe, no matter how small or how large, is always changing.

Movement and change are fundamental to everything that happens. You are changing right now. Everything you read affects you and causes you to experience mental change as your brain interprets the words you read. Your mind accumulates data and you react to the information. As you agree with or object to the data, you experience a change in your thought process and the amount of information within your immediate grasp. There is a change occurring within you right at this moment.

Every breath you take produces a change within you. Every word and noise you hear causes a change in your life. You, as a dynamic spiritual creature, are an ever-changing entity traveling throughout the macro universe. You are traveling through space at thousands of miles an hour on the vehicle we call earth. Everything in the universe is moving and evolving into something else. Change happens always, everywhere, and with everyone. There is rapid change, such as when a bomb drops on a city and blows everything to smithereens. And there is a slow change, such as what you go through as you age. It happens throughout the world, throughout outer space, and in every galaxy in existence. The sun that heats our planet is changing and will burn out in a few hundred million or a thousand billion years. Change is happening within your body and soul every moment. It is happening throughout the subatomic world, where tiny particles collide with one another and morph into ever-new forms of energy. Everything in the universe is in a constant state of change. You might even say that the only thing that does not change is the idea that movement and change are eternal.

With the first breath you take, you inhale spiritual energy from the environment that surrounds you. Some of this spiritual energy combines with your spiritual self. Some of it enters the so-called physical part of your body. Also, in every moment of your existence as a human being, you are shedding a minute amount of your soul, which rejoins with universal spiritual energy. You are shedding minute aspects of your strength, intelligence, wisdom, memory, and knowledge every moment. And you are also gaining subtle elements of strength, intelligence, learning, memory, and understanding every moment.

It is essential to understand that each cell's vibration rate in your body is continuously changing. Each cell is fast or slowly growing closer to or separating itself from its adjoining cells. Over a great deal of time, your cells discontinue operating in harmonic unison, your physical body breaks down, and you experience the deterioration of your biological cells. They return to their spiritual forms. As you age, your metabolism misfires and speeds up and slows down, causing separation and mistakes to happen throughout your cellular body. Your body undergoes damage from free radicals cruising through your veins. The free radicals mess with your DNA. Then, your physical cells continue to vibrate on a journey to reorganize as spiritual cells.

You are going through some kind of change every moment of your existence. When you sleep, the cells in your body, although vibrating, are also resting. They receive fresh energy to enable them to perform the chores they do for you every day. When you eat food, you take in the power that coordinates with your cells in such a way as to help you build up strength and feel healthy. Talking, meditating, dancing, walking, running, moving, hugging, singing, crying, laughing, and anger all create change. Although some people worry about climate change, the climate is always changing because it is natural. You, with your words, thoughts, and emotions, affect yourself and others, and others affect you. Genuine change is always happening and we should appreciate it.

There Are Many Types of Change

During your time in your physical body, you will go through all kinds of changes. Outside forces cause external change, such as people related to you, your friends, enemies, teachers, governments, and even objects smashing into your space. Words you hear cause internal change. Your thoughts and the foods you ingest will cause internal change. We can experience surprise change, natural change, unnatural change, self-directed change, forced change, beneficial change, harmful change, and other change types. Whatever we think, say, or do will cause change to occur within our being. The simple movement or vibration of every spiritual cell causes a universal change at every moment throughout eternity. One of the most beautiful and potentially thrilling aspects of our time spent on the physical plane is bringing improvement to ourselves, mentally, physically, or emotionally. Change always affects our spiritual essence.

When we truly focus on bringing the right type of change to ourselves and do it regularly, we can learn to do it with harmony and grace. Focusing on a fulfilling future for ourselves is essential in both the physical and spiritual realms. Our time spent on earth is a fantastic time for us to prepare for our future spiritual existence. When we spend most of our time in an unhappy mood, we prepare ourselves to spend our future time, whether in the physical or spiritual realm, in various unhappiness levels.

There are uncountable levels of emotions, ranging from utmost despair to delirious joy. Most people have periods of happiness to various degrees and periods of neutrality, sadness, or anger. Our moods continuously change. When we can achieve a default level of joy in our feelings, we tend to be healthy, happy, and prosperous. When our default level is feeling unhappy, defensive, threatening, or angry, we tend not to be successful. People make poor, lousy, stupid, and mean-spirited mistakes when they are sad or angry. When we are calm or happy, we make good or excellent decisions. Still, cheerful people sometimes make terrible decisions, and unhappy people occasionally make wise decisions. Unhappiness can also push a soul to change their worldly thought and activity. Despair often drives people to look inward to find a better life.

When we transition to a purely spiritual state, we carry with us our ability to communicate, process information, and feel. We also tend to forget much of what we experienced on earth. When we are born into the physical world, we forget everything about the spiritual world. It is just like in this life; it is difficult to remember what you were doing three or four years in the past at a specific time on a specific date. During our so-called physical life, our emotions and feelings are more intense than those we experience during our purely spiritual existence. Our physical life is a beautiful opportunity for us to develop the spiritual strength necessary to experience love, joy, and happiness during our strictly spiritual reality. Or, if you want to feel angry and upset all the time, your time on earth will give you every opportunity. It is your choice.

We Are Responsible for How We Handle Change

We are responsible for the way we feel; no one else is. When other people criticize or harm you, and you resent them, you give them control of your feelings. You allow them to control you rather than taking control of yourself. One of the first steps in developing spiritual happiness is to refuse to let other people control your thoughts and feelings. You make this change over time by directing the focus of your thoughts. When you focus on developing inner happiness, healthy body strength, and ideas that bring you success and satisfaction, you take control of how you change. Sure, there may be periods of your life on earth when it seems like everyone you know, and everyone you meet, is out to hurt you. Experiencing a dark night of the soul can be a challenging time, but you have the power to overcome the hurt.

Many people hurt so badly that they do harmful and stupid things to escape the pain. They may even harm or destroy themselves and bring their physical life to an end and enter the spiritual life once more. When they do this, they cause a great deal of change, but carry the lessons they need to learn right along with them. They will continue to face similar obstacles in the spiritual realm. They must still absorb the information they need to achieve happiness or whatever they need to take away their hurt. Pain is not just physical. It is also emotional, mental, and spiritual, and when you experience it, your soul experiences it. The change you experience will continue in a different time, manner, and place. Your level of hurt will also vary with every moment you experience it.

You, your body, your mind, and your spiritual essence will continue to experience change every moment throughout eternity. The universe we exist in is composed of vibrating energy. In its fully expanded state, there is nothing but vibrating energy. Fully expanded, the universe will radiate with love, peace, and varying levels of joy. The expanded universe is the time of heaven or Nirvana, of which various religions speak. The universe is in a continual state of expansion and shrinkage. When the universe is in its smallest state, all energy becomes compressed into a tiny, dense ball. When the universe expands, it snowballs. It forms giant gas clouds, planets, and many ever-evolving forms of matter. As worlds develop, physical energies develop from the invisible or spiritual essence. These energies in our world have evolved into many life-forms, including plants, animals, and human beings.

Change forces decisions

A child is born after spending approximately nine months in its mother's womb. Then, throughout the next months and years, it develops the abilities to walk, talk, feed itself, and understand what is happening around it. As the child ages, it continuously takes on spiritual and physical energy from the nutrients it consumes and the air it breathes. It also takes on feelings and information from the emotions and all energies it encounters. The acquisition of energy continues while the child matures and grows old. As the physical body ages, the energies that propel it continue to go through changes until the physical body breaks down. Its cells can no longer vibrate in harmony with the other cells of the body. The spiritual aspect of the body moves out into the larger universe. Even though the physical body's cells still vibrate, the body loses its ability to function as a human being and eventually turns back into purely spiritual energy.

Our changes cause us to grow more in harmony with universal energy or they can cause us to grow out of balance with universal life during our time on earth. As children, we spend a lot of time confused about how to feel and what to think. We even have confusion about how to act in many situations. As we move through life on earth, we need to learn to relax, love and deal harmoniously with people. As we re-enter our spiritual existence, we should be more in harmony with the universal whole than when we took on human form. However, many people abuse their time on earth and regress to existing as very unhappy, mean, or hurtful souls.

Forced change can enter our realities in many ways. A common way is when someone who wants to have power over others befriends them, gets control over their lives, and then mistreats them. An example of this is when a man treats a woman exceptionally well and entices her to depend on him, and possibly marries her. When she becomes dependent on him, he then abuses her emotionally and (or) physically. She loses faith in herself, becomes intimidated by him, and remains unhappy until she, out of desperation, flees the relationship. Some women stay in the relationship until they return to their spiritual existence. They keep their propensity to enter toxic relationships.

Anything or anyone can cause change

Men can also experience this type of situation under the influence of a woman or another man. Parents treat their children similarly to how their parents treated them when they were young. Depending on the child's sensitivity, this can produce beautiful results or a disaster where the child has enormous mental and emotional problems to overcome. It can happen to anyone. We continue to experience similar emotions in the spiritual universe that we experience on earth until we actively change or remove ourselves from the environment that causes our pain.

Another example of forced change is a change caused by the government. The government is often the most significant obstacle for people who want to improve their spiritual well-being. The people in government tell the general population that something is wrong, and that the government is there to help them. So, the people support the government. Then, the government leaders do nothing for the people but steal their money through taxation which they use to divide the population. Or they start wars and force the people to fight them, which creates fear and hate while the ruling class continues to tell the general population that it is helping it. It is challenging to create an environment of love and joy when the people in power want to keep their power more than they want to elevate themselves or anyone else.

Forced change comes from known and unknown sources. Parents, siblings, children, trusted friends, fellow workers, strangers, governments, climates, one's health, and even your financial situation can force change. If you can't pay your rent, someone may force you to move. Trusted friends might betray you and leave you in a difficult situation. You may do something illegal, either on purpose or by accident, and get arrested and put in jail, which might cause you a great deal of unhappiness.

Surprise change comes from unexpected sources, unhappy people, cheerful people, climate, governments, the universe, and the solar system. It can come from anywhere. You can walk down a path, and a rock can fall on your head and damage you in such a manner that you spend time in a hospital. A single accident can lead to you losing your job. You may accidentally meet a wonderful person who benefits your physical life. Every change you go through is an opportunity for you to learn how to experience love, wisdom, and happiness throughout your physical and spiritual being.

Through their own experience, some people feel they are better than other people or are smarter than other people and may control how others live. These people will tell you how they will take care of you and make your life a living joy. They may even criticize people who are wealthier or healthier than you and tell you how they will make it so you are more fit or more affluent than others. Beware of these people because when they get control of your life and happiness, they may not be as loving and helpful as they painted themselves. When they come into power, they will take from the rich just like a fabled Robin Hood did, but they won't give to the poor. They just keep it. Any large, powerful government is an example of this. These people take away your power to fend for yourself. The only way you can bring true happiness and well-being to yourself is through your own effort. Stand up to your difficulties and remove them from your life. When you do, it is a beautiful learning experience that helps you develop self-confidence and self-value.

Change Happens

Over 90 percent of the things that happen to us have their origins in our conscious and unconscious thoughts. There is a cause-and-effect relationship, though we might not always recognize it. A typical story of change is the deeply loved little child coddled through her childhood. She is an obedient child and does well in her school classes and, when she becomes an adult, expects to do well in everything she does. But the loving parents who were so protective of her forgot to teach her how to take care of herself. She gets out on her own and takes a job in another city that enables her to pay for a place to live. She is excited about her life and begins making new friends. The friends are delightful and introduce her to many of the so-called pleasures of life that her parents had always protected her from.

She soon starts taking drugs along with her newfound friends. Then she drives the car while her new boyfriend goes into a drugstore and robs it. Well, he gets caught by the police, and our beautiful, innocent young lady gets arrested as an accessory to the crime. Naturally, she becomes devastated. Change has hit her like a fist to the mouth. Being arrested allows her to make a choice. She can learn from her experience and become better at deciding about who she wants to associate with, or she can decide that there is nothing she can do to improve her life and continue to associate with the type of people who made unwise decisions about their own lives. When we refuse to accept or adapt to change, we inhibit our spiritual development and invite difficult changes for ourselves. We can change in helpful ways, or we can make things worse. To figure out how we can improve our situation, it takes deep thought and acceptance that our lives can improve. Then we must act.

We are on a far better footing spiritually and physically when we assume responsibility for what is happening in our life. When you focus on the good, the joyful, and success, chances are you will eventually achieve them. There is a saying, "Where your attention goes, your energy flows." It is true. When you focus on the situations you want in your life, you subconsciously look for ways to achieve them. You make decisions that bring you ever closer to your desired state. Admittedly, it may take months or years, depending on how far you are from where you want to be and what you want to be.

Random Chaos Causes Change

Chance is like luck. Luck is when preparation meets opportunity, they say. And that is the truth. Start positive change in your life regularly, and chance and fate will favor you. Ten-year-old Teddy Phillips was swimming in a public swimming pool one beautiful, warm summer day when he suddenly felt a sharp pain in the top of his head. His head hurt so badly that he swam over to the side of the pool to get out and rest. As he was climbing out of the pool, another young person told him that his head was bleeding. Teddy didn't know what had happened or what to do. Luckily for him, an adult saw what had happened and took Teddy to the hospital. Luckily again for Teddy, he needed only a couple of stitches to close the wound. What had happened was another child had been throwing rocks into the air and watching them hit the water. He didn't know Teddy and had no intention of hurting anyone. If you look out into the cosmos, you will see worlds colliding, shooting stars, and all kinds of chaos. It is neither good nor bad; it is just how the universe operates. Everyone will experience crises at different times in their life. Marriages break up, businesses fail, and death happens in the family. We lose our jobs, have significant health issues, or get wiped out financially. While crises are never enjoyable, they are almost always transformational. Why? Because the situation forces us to make changes we never would have made before the crisis. Comfort is the enemy of change. When we are too comfortable in our present situation, we often resist the impulse to make a change. A crisis dramatically forces that change upon us. It is almost always painful and rarely pleasant. Still, if accepted as an opportunity to create something new, it is ultimately healing and nearly always beneficial. You can trust the process of crises.

Movement and change are the order, meaning, and business of the universe. They last forever. Positive change produces more positive change, and negative change begets more negative change. There are three leading causes of change in our lives: chance, choice, and crisis. All three are powerful and cause different results. Chance brings change to you in ways you are not expecting. Someone might give you a million dollars, or someone else might steal a thousand dollars from you. You weren't expecting either one, but both circumstances bring you new opportunities with which to deal. Some may be easy and pleasurable, and others may be terrifying. A crisis introduces chance. It always calls for some kind of instant action that can either improve your state of being or bring hurt and fear into your life.

Whether given to you by someone else or self-directed, all choices are powerful because they allow you to aim toward what you want to accomplish. As you travel your self-directed path, you might encounter chances and crises along the way, but you will have an eventual goal for which to work. With your self-directed plan, you become in control of the direction of your physical life. Having control of your life is much more exciting and interesting than leaving your life to whatever comes up next. When you set a goal to accomplish something that will benefit you or someone else, you create a fantastic choice for your actions. When you visualize your success in achieving your goal, you design how you will accomplish it. When you take control, you have a self-directed choice.

Change is everywhere and constant—everything changes. Even the way we communicate is continually changing. We invent new words and discontinue using words. We share not only through our words but also our handwriting, our actions, and our emotions. Emotion is the universal language.

THOUGHTS

- Change is constant, everywhere, and forever
- You experience change every moment of your life
- Your emotions and physical health constantly change
- Your physical life can improve your spiritual life
- You are responsible for your thoughts and feelings
- Hurtful emotions breed hurtful actions
- Positive emotions breed positive actions
- Change often comes from unknown sources
- It is your responsibility to react to change appropriately

CHAPTER 5

THE LANGUAGE OF THE UNIVERSE

Many people believe human beings are superior to all other physical creatures because humans have thumbs and can talk. The thumbs are helpful, but all animals can talk. Many creatures and even non creatures communicate with each other. It is relatively easy to see animals communicating with one another. We see dogs playing with each other, sometimes arguing with each other, acting happy as if in celebration, and even taking care of each other. You can see ants working together to protect their homes and search for food and new homes in which to live. Sometimes when a human is very sick, the pet they live with won't leave their side. The animal knows the human is ill and wants to do what it can do to help. How do bugs, spiders, fish, birds, and all other forms of energy communicate? They communicate through the most powerful and accurate language in the universe—the language of emotions and feelings.

Our spiritual energy is continually communicating with other spiritual life. We express feelings, sensations, and emotions, such as love, anger, rejection, and acceptance. When humans first walked around the earth, they either had no vocal cords or rudimentary ones. In fact, psychologists now say that we convey only seven percent of our messages with words. We communicate the remaining ninety-three percent through our tone of voice and body language. Early humans could grunt and make other sounds, but mainly communicated with their emotions, psychic energy, intuition, body language, and physical expression. They expressed themselves much like the way many animals communicate today. This type of communication was just as useful for the so-called caveman as our spoken language is today.

As human vocal cords developed, humankind gave meaning to the sounds, and soon we had language. Different languages developed in different regions of the world because people gave different meanings to the sounds they uttered. As language evolved, humankind began using it more and more to communicate. We learned to talk to one another and developed the ability to write and spell words to form sentences. With the increased use of language, communication through emotional energy, psychic ability, and intuition receded. Humans often attempt to block emotional expression in favor of using the spoken language during our present time. This form of communication is efficient, but often cannot convey the true meaning of the message. In fact, people frequently misunderstand what someone is saying to them. There is a game people sometimes play. A group of people get together, and one person whispers a few words to the person next to them. That person passes it along to the next person and on down the line. The last person to receive the secret then speaks the message they got out loud. Often, the last message differs from the original message. Using language to communicate allows the speaker to deceive others and lie about various topics. They don't even have to lie. People often just don't understand what they hear. Feelings and emotions are much more honest and direct.

People used to say that animals and other varieties of life lacked intelligence. "Dumb animal" is still often used when describing various animals. But when your puppy comes up to you, lies down on its back, spreads out its legs, and starts wagging its tail, you can be pretty sure it wants you to scratch it. When the animal does something they shouldn't, and you find out, the animal acts guilty. It wants you to forgive it. After you punish them a few times, they will stop the behavior of which you disapprove. Animals are not stupid; they are intelligent and talk with each other just as humans do.

Emotions Are Spiritual

The universe is composed of energy—atomic particles, dark matter, dark energy, protons, photons, quarks, leptons, gluons, muons, and lots of other tiny, tiny particles existing in fields. There is little thought about how these energy particles communicate with one another—or if they do. Spiritual energy communicates telepathically, psychically, and through vibratory energy. The organs of your body communicate the same way. Information is passed directly from organ to organ or through the nervous system. Your body functions twenty-four hours a day. Even though you do not notice it, your cells are in continual communication. Your fingers connect to your hands, which attach to your wrists, which move in tandem. Your legs connect with your hips, and they must cooperate for your body to function correctly. You don't notice all the activity in your body because you do not need to. Your limbs and your cells inherently know how to do their jobs, just as you know how to swallow food. In fact, the seventy-five trillion cells in your body cooperate much better than the eight billion people living on earth. While your body is working to keep you healthy and viable in human form, you continually experience feelings of happiness, sadness, love, and a whole range of emotions. These feelings are what you take with you throughout eternity.

When you meet a fellow human being in the physical universe, you sometimes get a feeling of warmth or one of mistrust. Your spiritual, emotional self is communicating with you. As you get to know the person better, your feelings toward them may increase in either a positive or negative manner. You are subconsciously trading information with the other person. Suppose you mentally and emotionally feel uncomfortable around them. In that case, it is a strong warning that there is something amiss in your relationship, and you need to be careful. You may ignore this warning because someone taught you to disregard your emotions. Conversely, suppose you become comfortably attached to someone emotionally, mentally, and physically, and they feel the same about you. In that case, you are likely to have a long-term beneficial relationship. The more you listen to your emotions, the more you will understand their meaning.

You may have had a psychic reading by someone who claims to have the power to tell you about your future or past. During that reading, the reader may have laid cards down on a table and claimed to be reading them, or perhaps they held your hands and started talking about your life. Sometimes these readings are accurate, especially when the reader takes hold of your hands. The reader is feeling your emotions. You tell the reader what to say to you through your feelings, emotions, and responses—whether verbal or physical.

Most people like to be hugged at certain times, if not all the time. Hugs are powerful. If you have embraced many people, you may have noticed that some people are warm, soft, gentle, and very comforting when they hug. In contrast, others hug you like they are a piece of wood and only touch a tiny part of your body. The difference is one type of hug is very open and very pleasurable to the one doing the hug. In contrast, the other one is guarded and does not want to expose themselves to anything they may be nervous about. There is nothing wrong with either type of hug. It is like speaking different words. They give out differing messages.

Anger is easy to recognize

You walk into a party and immediately become overwhelmed by the smell of wonderfully fragrant chocolate chip cookies. The scent is drifting from the cookies to your nose, and your olfactory neurons pick up the aroma. The cookies are physical, and your nose is physical, as are your olfactory neurons. The smell of the cookies is not material. It is not solid. It is invisible or spiritual energy. You cannot feel the aroma, and you can't see it. The only reason you recognize it is because you can smell it. When you stand where you can see the cookies, you can identify them as cookies. But it is not a physical process, and it is the energy of the cookies that gives you the smell. Even though energy and matter are the same, they are different forms of the same vibrating substance and still can communicate with you.

You pick up a cookie, and it feels solid. You are not touching the cookie. We never touch anything, considering 99.99 percent of every atom in the cookie is empty space. When you hold on to it, the feeling of solidness comes from the resistance of electrons in the cookie. Electrons have no mass. Science tells us they are non-dimensional particles of negative electrical charge that surround atoms and molecules. They are spiritual energy. As you hold the cookie, your grasp forces its electrons to speed up. The speeding up requires energy from your hand. This energy delivers a message to your brain, which interprets it as touching something tangible. It is only an illusion that we live in a world with solid bodies and objects.

We are spiritual beings living in a spiritual universe. When you walk outside on a beautiful, sunshiny day, you can observe the sun shining down on you. The sun generates light through nuclear fusion and converts about four million tons of matter into energy every second. It blasts particles of spiritual or electrical energy toward earth as light. Emotions are also invisible or spiritual significance. Our feelings are a spiritual language in that they are always talking to us and giving us information. This information might be about our surroundings. It might be about other people, animals, events in our lives, or anything you can imagine. Emotions interconnect with thought and our physical bodies. They affect our thoughts, health, relationships, decisions, activities, and everything we experience in life.

Your emotions are always in sync with your thoughts. Thoughts of happy times or events make you satisfied, and thoughts of unfortunate events or times make you feel sad, unhappy, or angry. You emotionally express your thoughts and feelings, although some people do their best to hide their feelings. By using emotion and reason together, we can improve our success and happiness. Our emotions are contagious. They copy the feelings of those close to us, and those close to us often incorporate the feelings we generate. People unconsciously use smiles to show other people they are friendly and not a threat. When someone silently expresses anger, it is easy to recognize.

Even Animals pick up emotions

There is a massive communication system throughout the universe. Understandably, you don't know about everything going on in the universe or your country, state, home, even in your own body. But the communication is there. Even though they are universal, emotions are personal. They project what we're feeling to those around us, whether or not we want them to. Emotions are also interpersonal. Another person's show of emotion usually triggers a reaction from us—perhaps support if the person is a close friend or awkwardness if the person is a stranger. Emotions are central to any interpersonal relationship.

Emotions are physiological, behavioral, and communicative reactions to stimuli that are cognitively processed and experienced. That is a high falutin sentence stating the fact that they simply broadcast reality. Studies have shown that body language and emotional delivery contribute anywhere from 55 to 90 percent of understanding in any communication between two or more people. Feelings state the truth. Negative emotions cause stress. Positive emotions cause joy and happiness. Stress can kill people or help them improve their health. Too much stress can cause cancer and other diseases. Too little stress can cause ennui or listlessness. When athletes train to develop their physical bodies, they stress their muscles to teach them to withstand ever-increasing pressures.

Our emotions provide information to others that tells them how they should react. For example, when someone we care about displays behavior associated with sadness, we are likely to become sad along with them and know that we need to support them. Emotions help us read information from others and help us send information to them. Primary emotions are innate feelings experienced for short periods that appear rapidly, usually because of an outside stimulus. We experience them similarly across cultures. Typical emotions are joy, love, distress, anger, fear, surprise, guilt, shame, embarrassment, pride, envy, jealousy, hunger, and disgust. Members of a remote tribe in New Guinea never exposed to Westerners identified these raw emotions when shown photographs of Americans making corresponding facial expressions.

Animals pick up our emotions. Dogs and cats understand them. They even communicate with humans emotionally. Baby birds in unhatched eggs have a sense of awareness. Researchers from the University of Vigo in northwestern Spain found that the tiny baby birds inside their eggs can hear warning squawks from adult gulls. When they listen to them, they will delay hatching until the immediate threat passes. Even trees actively choose the type of fungi and bacteria they deal with in the soil. Depending on the earth's decomposition rate, the trees will decide which fungi they will partner with. Yes, trees, just like everything else in the universe, produce information for surrounding energies to interpret.

Emotions Tell Who You Are

A key element in humanity's continuation and success has been our ability to group together and develop interpersonal bonds. The ability to express emotions has played a significant role in this success. Empathy allows us to share the emotional state of someone else and increases interpersonal bonding. These capacities were critical as early human society grew increasingly complex, and people needed to live with other humans.

People seek happy situations and strive to communicate positive emotions, even when they do not feel positive emotions. Being positive implicitly states that you have achieved your personal goals and have a comfortable life. It also broadcasts that you know what you are doing, have confidence, and are a winner. The ability to understand feelings helps you succeed when communicating with other people. When you are emotionally aware, you communicate better. You notice and understand other people's emotions, and you understand that how they feel influences how they communicate. You also understand the meaning of what they say to you and why they say it.

Bill Williamson was a siding salesman. The first, and possibly one of the best lessons he learned in his sales career, was to ask for the sale six times before he gave up. This approach sounds pushy, but there was sound reasoning behind it. The people he was selling to wanted to buy his product, but they didn't trust salespeople, did not listen to what they said, and needed lots of help in making tough decisions. For this reason, whenever he made a sales call, he would talk to his clients for a little while, and then make an excuse to leave to get something out of his car. After a few minutes, he would come back. The reasoning for this was the first time they saw him he was a stranger, and the second time, they were friends—a small psychological trick to help him get the trust of his clients. He would ask for the sale several times for his clients to get used to the idea of having new siding. After the first no, he would change the subject and talk for another five to fifteen minutes before asking for the sale again. By the time he did this several times, it often became a foregone conclusion to his clients that they wanted the siding and that they would buy the siding.

As a side note, Bill was sincere and very proud of his job and the company he worked for, and he knew he was selling a high-quality product. He worked for the company for about a year until one of his customers told him he wanted the siding, but asked him to hold off for three days before installing it. He needed to check with his financial adviser to ensure the funds were available to pay cash for it. Bill agreed and turned in the paperwork for the job. The next day, he got a phone call from his customer unhappily telling him to take the siding off his house. Bill was shocked because he had communicated to the people he worked for that he had assured his customer they would wait for three days before beginning the job. The people who owned the company Bill worked for told him that they always start the job immediately so the customer can't back out. This devastated Bill. He felt he had lied to his customer and felt humiliated. He went home and stayed there for a week, not doing anything. He was so depressed, he thought about killing himself. He never went back to work for that company. Slowly he realized he needed to go back to work, and he got a job selling vacuum cleaners. He never again even thought about selling siding. The way the situation affected Bill is an example of just how powerful our emotions can be.

Emotions speak

Have you ever tried to hide your feelings? Like when you are very upset with someone but do not want them to know it, and you must talk to them face-to-face? It's difficult for most people and impossible for others. That is because emotions don't lie, and you experience them whether you want to or not. Instead of hiding or ignoring your feelings and the feelings of others, focus on them and endeavor to understand what they say. Your understanding of emotions will help you improve your communication ability.

People have been classifying and discussing emotions for years with little success. All feelings are normal and natural. They play an essential role in our lives. Some are more pleasant than others, but that doesn't mean that we should avoid the less pleasant ones or seek to suppress our emotions. Doing so might have adverse effects on our mental, emotional, and physical well-being. Emotions are the universal form of communication and help us communicate with and understand others. The Merriam Webster Dictionary defines emotions as "a conscious mental reaction (such as anger or fear) subjectively experienced as strong feeling usually directed toward a specific object and typically accompanied by physiological and behavioral changes in the body." In other words, emotions are a type of language. People do not universally accept the truth of that statement.

Your Emotions Stay in Sync with Your Thoughts

Emotions express everything we need to say. Happiness is the most universally recognized of all emotions. It shows contentment, pleasure, and good cheer. In all cultures, people express joy by smiling, laughing, and being energetic. When we feel happy, we share with others by approaching them and connecting with them. When this occurs, it often makes the other person happy, resulting in an enjoyable social experience. Research shows that being happy reduces our stress, thus contributing to overall health and well-being. Love is a universal expression. When you like something, you show it in your emotions. When you are unhappy, disgusted, angry, or feel contempt for something or someone, other people can spot your feelings quickly and easily. Since our bodies are adept at using spoken language and easily control the words we speak, we use speech to communicate. It is easy to lie using speech but difficult to lie using emotions.

It is important to remember that our emotions are contagious. One interesting characteristic of emotions is that other people's emotions can control and deplete ours. Modern man has invented such phenomena as television, movies, computers, and the radio, which can aid our communication with one person or a group of people worldwide. Many of the people and groups of people who use these inventions do so for devious means. An example of this is when one person on television criticizes someone else. He could be lying about the other person and vilifying him or her. Because he dislikes that person, the people watching him may also oppose the criticized person without even thinking about it. They digest the emotions of the speaker and develop similar feelings. If you follow politics, where two sides brag about themselves and criticize the other side, the people who support them often act in the same manner.

When the meanest, cruelest, most dishonest politicians produce the strongest emotion, their communication recipients subconsciously develop the same anger without knowing why. This is one facet of communication that complicates the honest character of our feelings. When we can understand this, we can understand that those people are mean-spirited or unhappy themselves. It improves our ability to judge their character. One of the significant reasons for living in the physical realm is to enhance our ability to experience peace and happiness unless you want to be a jerk or a sourpuss. Then go at it. You will carry your emotional default level with you when you transition to the purely spiritual plane.

Humankind has developed many new ways to communicate, such as telephone, television, internet, and radio. These communication forms help us send our words, pictures, and emotions to other people a great distance from ourselves. Your feelings are always in sync with your thoughts. Emotions are related to the views of the mind at each moment. Thoughts of happy times or events make you satisfied, and thoughts of unfortunate events or times make you feel sad or angry. You always emotionally express your thoughts and feelings, although some people work very hard to hide their feelings. By using emotion and reason together, we can improve our success and happiness. Our emotions are contagious, as our cells copy the emotions of those close to us, but when we maintain our composure and cheerful attitude, we often overpower the negative feelings of others. In fact, we can counter the energy thieves who enter our lives. People will inevitably come into our lives as energy thieves or psychic vampires.

THOUGHTS

- Emotions are a universal form of communication
- Emotions perpetually communicate the truth
- Psychiatrists say only seven percent of communication is verbal
- Humankind spoke with emotions and gestures before words
- Your soul speaks with you through your emotions
- Your pets can understand what you want from them
- You are spiritual energy using a physical body
- You have many ways to communicate
- Your emotions stay in sync with your thoughts

CHAPTER 6

ENERGY THIEVES AND PSYCHIC VAMPIRES

Have you ever spent time with someone who wears you out emotionally and physically? Have you had an acquaintance who would comment about how sick you look or how dreadful something is or pour out their own sad story when you talked to them for longer than five or ten minutes? If so, the odds are you were in the presence of an energy thief. A better label for this type of person is *psychic vampire.*

You can recognize that you are in the presence of a psychic vampire when your warm, pleasant conversation turns unhappy, depressing, or angry. You develop a feeling of empathy for who you are talking to initially, but after a few minutes, you feel depressed and even become physically exhausted for no apparent reason. Whiners are a common type of psychic vampire, and there are several more types you are likely to deal with while you spend your time in human form. Have you ever been in a conversation with someone who keeps talking and talking, and you find you can hardly get a word in edge wise? You might even have a hard time ending the conversation because they just keep droning on. They keep talking about something you are not even interested in every time you attempt to leave. Yep! That is another type of energy thief. This type might even invade your physical space to get closer to you than comfortable for you.

Narcissistic Vampires

Narcissistic people are one type of energy thief. They feel they are superior to others. They are controllers and refuse to admit that they ever make mistakes or are wrong. Nothing is ever their fault, and if you don't do as they tell you to do, Katy bar the door. Perhaps the narcissist is the sneakiest type of psychic vampire. They will befriend you and be exceptionally friendly with you until they gain your confidence as a trusted friend. Then they slowly start demanding that you do things for them.

If you do not escape their friendship reasonably quickly, you become no better than their slave, and they will treat you like one. And when you attempt to end the relationship, they will point out everything they have done for you in the past. You become the bad guy, especially if you have empathy for others. These energy thieves can be vicious when they believe they have been wronged and can do you actual harm physically, mentally, and spiritually. Their ultra niceness, in the beginning, can be a clue. Often it is unnatural. They will be very kind, thoughtful, and caring in the first part of your relationship. They will do things they believe will convince you to become dependent on them. After they gain your trust and loyalty, they take advantage of you. They become abusive and treat you like you are less than a human and act as if they are the king of the world. Many empathic people become entrapped in this type of situation for years.

Drama Queens

There is also the drama queen. This type of person exaggerates everything. If they sneeze, they think they are going to die. If you don't notice a new chair in their living room, they will accuse you of being rude and uncaring. They will go on and on about how they are unloved and unappreciated and how nothing ever goes their way. They feel sorry for themselves, and it becomes your job to make them feel better. And it gets harder and harder to make them feel better. When you spend a few hours with them, they will become rather happy. However, you will feel totally drained of energy, possibly even lifeless. They did their job, and it somehow pleased them.

With these energy drainers, there is one common denominator. Their reality is correct and essential, and you are not. You are there to provide the energy for them to drain. It is imperative to recognize that you're only necessary to their life to drain your energy. If you are not there to listen to them, they will find someone who will. A relationship with an energy drainer is a learning experience that many people endure for years.

Anyone can be an energy thief. Many people who become psychic vampires only do so after they experience trauma in their life. An example is someone whose spouse leaves them after taking all their savings. The person left behind deeply hurts and shares their problems with everyone they know. Some of these people never recover. They hurt badly, and they repeat their story to whomever will listen. It becomes habitual. They have very few friends at any one time, and the people who befriend them move away from them fairly quickly.

The psychic vampire will often revert to their history of being normal after a few weeks or months when they realize what they are doing, or someone sets them straight. These are not necessarily intentionally bad people. They were just hit with an unfortunate situation. In any relationship you have with these people, your spiritual essence is experiencing the same trauma as they are. The energy thief is pulled to you because he or she subconsciously recognizes something about your spiritual nature that is open to attack. Or they see something in you that appeals to them, and they want to be like you. It is often a lesson you need to learn to bring you closer to nirvana or spiritual happiness.

You can meet an energy thief at any time in your physical life, and it may take a while to figure out just what they are doing. In fact, they might not even realize what they are doing. One of the easiest ways to recognize a psychic vampire is to understand that they believe they are always right. They think their opinions are important and matter, no matter with whom they associate. Let's say you feel good and happily greet your vampire. He or she takes one look at you and says, "Oh my gosh. You look terrible. Are you okay?" You respond you are fine and continue the conversation. After a few minutes, you leave, and your *friend* tells you, "I hope you feel better." If you are suggestible, this could lead to you becoming sick, and your vampire will enjoy experiencing your pain. Your vampire friend may even offer to help you.

Refuse to Tolerate Vampirism

The best way to stop this treatment is to tell them you do not want them to speak to you like that. Tell them to ask you how you feel rather than telling you that you look sick, and you will tell them how you feel. They don't realize that whatever they say to you, their spiritual essence also hears it and thinks they are talking to it. They teach themselves to be a more potent energy sucker. The vampire not only tries to pull you down but also unconsciously pulls him or herself down. But being down doesn't disturb your vampire. The energy thief seldom feels good or experiences happiness unless he or she exercises control or is at least a powerful influence on someone else's behavior.

When in a so-called loving relationship, the thief will overreact to minor annoyances. The vampire will get angry over something as mundane as someone failing to buy something for them they had promised to buy. Or if it's a husband who comes home to find that dinner is not ready for him, he may explode at the wife. They have no compassion and cannot understand that their wishes and demands may not be the essential thing in the world. When you react to them to get them out of your life, you are helping yourself and them because you allow them to look within and change their behavior. Actually, the best way to let them know you dislike what they do to you is to tell them you do not appreciate their behavior. It is best to tell them in a calm, cordial manner and with a smile. If nothing else, this will send a signal that they have not upset you, you have your act together, and you are not angry at them. The first time you do this, it may be terrifying because very few people enjoy confrontation. But the more you do it, the easier it gets. It can be enjoyable telling your personal, spiritual truth in this manner. If the other person values your friendship or companionship, they may change and stop dumping on you. Either way, you are likely to be better off.

Marci had a relationship with a guy she felt was her twin flame. Her definition of twin flame was a high-level, soul-based connection for spiritual growth. The two previous weekends, they had argued when they were together. She decided they were no longer twin flames and wanted to end the relationship. He told her that her friends caused her to feel that way, and the relationship needed to continue. Marci was of sound mind and felt he was trying to control her. She calmly told him the relationship was over and she would have nothing to do with him anymore. Typical of energy suckers, her now ex-boyfriend refused to accept his role in the relationship's dissolution.

They may implore you to remain their friend, or they may shame you into continuing to stay with them, promising not to weigh you down with their problems anymore. But until this time, your only choice is to refuse to tolerate their behavior any longer. When you do this, you get rid of the psychic vampire. You energize your soul, freeing it up to continue its journey of preparing for an eternity of love and happiness. In fact, your intelligent and dignified assertiveness will help you prepare for your future spiritual life.

Susan's Experience

Another way to get rid of them is to ignore them. Susan became friends with Molly, who worked in the same company as she did. After they got to know each other, they began eating lunch together in the company cafeteria. Susan quickly learned that Molly was divorced. Molly's ex-husband, who used to treat her poorly, ran off with her sister. Molly was hurting because of how badly that rotten guy had treated her. Susan had a lot of empathy for her because she had had an unhappy relationship with someone herself. Susan felt good about listening to Molly at first, but it exhausted her after a few months. Every time she ate lunch with Molly, she would leave the table drained of energy. Molly was always happy after their lunch was over.

Susan slowly realized that Molly seemed to overdo her rant about her ex-spouse, so one day she asked her how long it had been since the divorce. Molly responded, "Fourteen years." Susan thought, *What? This is crazy! This lady has been divorced for fourteen years and is still blaming her ex-husband for ruining her life.* The meal was over, so they left, and Susan quickly decided that she would escape from Molly, though she didn't know how she would do it. She did not want to hurt Molly's feelings or make her mad because they worked together. Her way out of the relationship was to quit going to lunch with Molly. So, she started making excuses for why she couldn't go. Molly kept asking her to eat together for about two weeks. Then she stopped, and Susan never heard from her again. Molly was back looking for another person with whom she could share her sad stories.

They Can Make You Feel Guilty

Some energy thieves like to use guilt as a weapon to get what they want. "You won't go with me to see my cousin? I went with you to see your parents every time you went. I make the paycheck, so why can't you have dinner ready when I get here?" They will use anything to make their victim feel bad. After a time, it causes one to become frustrated. If there is bad news, the energy thief gets pleasure in being the first one to deliver it. Suppose there is a terrible storm anywhere in the world, or a terrorist attack in some large city. In that case, the psychic vampire will express their fear that whatever the disaster is, it could quickly destroy both of you. They like to get you stirred up about what may go wrong with your life. A highly suggestible person might succumb to their suggestions.

As stated earlier, the best way to deal with a psychic vampire is to ignore them. Stay away from them if possible. It is difficult to recognize an energy thief before you get to know them. In fact, they are usually pleasant when you first meet them. Some people can recognize them right out of the box, but these people are very much in tune with their spiritual essence. They have learned much about developing a happy and focused path to follow while on planet Earth.

When you realize you are dealing with one of these creatures, it is wise to set limits immediately on how much time you will spend with them. They will often talk you to death if you give them the opportunity. When you decide you want to get away from them, just stop reacting to their stories. They feed off your reactions and get subconscious pleasure when they manipulate your emotions. When you don't feel sorry for them or empathize with them or react with compassion, they leave reasonably quickly. They go off to find another victim. Stay upbeat when you are in the presence of an energy thief. Suppose you can keep the conversation directed calmly or happily. In that case, you might keep them from going into one of their dramatic acts. But you face the danger that they will get in a talking jag and bore you with some long tale in which you have no interest. It can be challenging to find a place to cut into their diatribe. The quickest way to stop them is to cut in quickly and tell them it is time for you to leave. Don't argue with them because they will resist and demand that you allow them to finish their meal, which is your emotional health.

Honesty and a Smile Are Helpful

Most people must deal with energy thieves at least once in their lifetime. They give you the opportunity to assert and develop your spiritual strength. You build up your spiritual power by learning how to deal with them. It might first be something like limiting the time you spend with them. The next step might be determining your availability to them. You can even spend time courteously explaining that they make you feel bad. Then politely tell them you will not tolerate it anymore. But when they continue to drag you down, there comes a time for you to tell them flat out they pull you down and you do not want to associate with them anymore. The person with well-developed spiritual muscle quickly recognizes the signs and treats the vampire with respect, but does not encourage or accept any whining, accusations, or judgments from them. When you develop to this extent, it can give you self-confidence and inner joy when you save yourself from one of these creatures' foibles.

Suppose you are a person who is growing spiritually. In that case, you will most likely attract a few psychic vampires in your development. You will also intimidate some of them. Some of them will sense that you are a feeling, empathic person, which you likely are, and they become attracted to you because they want what you have. You will continue to attract these kinds of people until you develop the spiritual strength to repel them. With each one you get rid of, you get stronger and wiser about how to handle them. When you have a high default level of emotional happiness, along with your strong self-confidence, you are likely to intimidate these people. They won't bother to get close to you anymore.

There are three potent forms of communication that you can develop that will help you repel, cure, or reject energy thieves. The first one is the smile, and the second is the phrase "I understand." The third one is blunt, happy, and friendly honesty and clarity about what you want from them. When you learn to make a smile in your default facial expression, you attract all kinds of people. Some will be friendly, some will be mean, and some may be extraordinary people. The smile is an advertising sign that says you are successful and a winner. It also broadcasts the idea that you are an open-minded, trustworthy, confident, and knowledgeable person. The smile will attract people. Many of them will even return your smile and carry it with them and smile at the next person or two they encounter. Some people will be terrified by your smile. They will be intimidated and feel that you know something that they don't know or that you are on some kind of higher plane of consciousness than they are. They will avoid you every chance they get.

You can help your vampires

Say you are speaking with someone. When the person tells you some story, whether beautiful or horrible, use the magic phrase "I understand" whether you understand or don't. This phrase is not a lie. If you don't know what they are talking about, you will realize what it is soon. You are telling them you acknowledge they are thinking about some experience they are expecting, wanting, or that has already happened. Telling them you understand will tend to calm them down. As an example, say they are complaining about their ex-spouse. You can say something like, "I understand. Many of us have been through similar circumstances. Now I want you to relax and respectfully tell me what you are going to do about it." Tell them how you want to be treated. If they complain or tell you another sad story, listen to whatever it is. Tell them you understand, and politely ask them to treat you with respect. Tell them you do not want to hear about their sad story; you want to hear how they will solve their problem. Or tell them you want to know how they will get out of their miserable mess. Do whatever it takes. Then be quiet and wait for their answer. Your response may very well completely throw them off base, or they might comply with your remarks. Taking charge of the conversion can be frightening the first few times you do it. But not only will you grow spiritually, you will also gain self-confidence.

If you want to be physically strong, you will experience muscle soreness while exercising your physical muscles. When you learn to deal with psychic vampires, you may have the spiritual strength to put up with them all day, but you, more than likely, will always deal with them quickly. You will not bother to put up with their abuse. If you're going to be spiritually healthy, you must exercise your spiritual power. If you are dealing with evil or nasty people, the best thing you can do is stay away from them. You must always protect yourself because you are here to develop your spiritual strength, and it is up to you to figure out precisely what you must do. You can say to yourself, "I am the one who must get it done." Your language does not have to be perfect and proper, but the thought and emotion need to be correct.

When you treat your psychic vampires in a manner that forces them to stop draining your energy or gets them out of your life, you not only help yourself, but you help them. You allow them to look within and change their behavior. They are spiritual beings just like you and are made of the same spiritual material in which you are composed. They are neither better nor worse than you. They are spiritual energy, just like you, only experiencing a different reality. You may exist with them in the future. When you develop your spiritual muscle properly, you will always create a proper environment for yourself and help others on their spiritual journey. You will become the embodiment of an expression of your soul.

THOUGHTS

- Anyone can be an energy thief
- Some people are psychic vampires for only a short time
- You will probably know at least one energy thief
- Beware of people who cause you to feel guilty
- Set your limits for what you will tolerate
- Honesty with a smile is powerful
- The phrase "I understand" is helpful in many situations
- You help vampires when you are honest with them
- Psychic vampires are spiritual beings just like you

CHAPTER 7
EXPRESS YOUR TRUE SPIRITUAL SELF

During your time on earth, you have the fantastic opportunity to set the basis for your future spiritual existence. You also continually have a tremendous opportunity to improve your life as a physical being. Most people drift along, reacting to whatever comes their way. Some people believe they have a purpose and spend their earthly life attempting to achieve it. In contrast, others spend their time figuring out their purpose. Some never think about having a purpose. Your goal is whatever you decide it to be.

We are spiritual creatures in a decidedly physical environment that continuously vibrates, moves, and changes. The atmosphere is ever changing, and we are constantly moving, vibrating, and going through some change. No matter our makeup, whether spiritual or physical, we experience emotions that can range from deep hatred to overflowing love. We will always have the power of thought and communication wherever we exist.

Whether or not you decide to have a purpose, you will be more in touch with your spiritual essence when you can honestly express your thoughts and emotions. The ideas you have and the words and feelings you express come directly from your soul, which is the container of your mind and the energy that contains your mind. Every tiny particle of your spiritual essence craves to express its feelings and wants. When you repress these desires, it causes stress throughout your body and mind. When you say them in a positive, loving manner, you contribute to your peace and happiness, and you benefit others who experience the healthy atmosphere you produce.

Dictionaries describe the mind as "the element of a person that enables them to be aware of the world and their experiences." They describe it as the faculty of consciousness and thought or, as a general term, the center of all mental activity. They say nothing about the spiritual or mental aspects, such as its relationship with your soul and universal spiritual energy. Sometimes they say the mind is housed in the brain and other parts of the body, but they do not describe it. That is because they don't know what it is. You have the faculty of thinking, feeling, and being conscious of everything around you. Scientists either haven't figured it out or can't bring themselves to admit it is the spiritual part of you we call the soul. Your mind is an essential part of your soul. The sounds you express reflect your spiritual energy. Speak with fear, and you are afraid in your energy, or in other words, your soul. When you speak with love and joy, you build up your spiritual self's ability to radiate love and happiness.

People tell other people what they think the other person wants to hear to get along with them. Going along to get along is not how one asserts their true self. You become assertive when you dare to speak your mind while being respectful of other people's boundaries. In fact, you can say almost anything to another person if you smile and talk politely. Do you want to be a slave to other people's desires and thoughts, or do you want to follow your dream? As was mentioned earlier, people go along to get along in part because they don't like change or confrontation. But this does not contribute to their spiritual growth. And spiritual growth is a fundamental reason for our existence on earth. Your time on earth is a training period to prepare for whatever dimension you enter when your time on earth ends.

Being Assertive Can Be Scary

The ability to express your true, honest feelings liberates you. It gives you the spiritual strength to feel powerful and happy. It is like an athlete training to excel in an athletic contest. When you train correctly, you improve and do well. When you don't prepare, you may not do so well. A person with a well-developed spiritual essence has high self-esteem and can assert their thoughts with love, gentleness, and authority. When we are on earth, we use words, verbal communication, or writing to communicate and get our ideas, wants, and needs across to others. These forms of communication can easily be deceptive. Most people speak to gain acceptance from others. Speaking to tell the exact truth can be terrifying in the beginning because other people might argue and criticize you for daring to be honest. Stop and think for a minute. Are you completely honest with every word you say? Do you occasionally allow people to misunderstand what you say to them? Do you even know if people understand what you say even when they act as they do? The amount of disharmony in the world results from tremendous misinformation, falsehood, and confusion. When you assert the truth the best you can and listen to your responses, you can be confident that the person you communicate with understands your message.

Misunderstanding of other people's ideas, thoughts, and feelings leads to a massive amount of trauma. It breeds anger and resentment and can lead to physical abuse. The better you can get your ideas and feelings across in a gentle, loving manner, the better off you will be in every area of your life.

When you express your thoughts, needs, and wants along with your true feelings diligently, you will lose some of your so-called friends. Losing friends is nothing to worry about because you make room for new and better friends. You will also lose your fear of hurting others. You will realize that anyone can use anything you say or do as an excuse to blame you for their feelings, which, in reality, you have no control over. How they respond to you is their business and not yours. You will quickly gain intestinal fortitude and spiritual strength. You will also feel better about yourself and increase your self-confidence.

You are the creator of your destiny. You can make it happy or sad, good or bad, loving, or hateful, successful, or an all-out losing proposition. When you become willing to express your opinions and desires, the universe hears your message and helps contribute to your wishes. When you cannot assert your feelings and desires, you are open to being the victim of other people's wants and desires. Asserting yourself does not mean blaming others for your decisions, conditions, well-being, or anything else. When you refuse to take responsibility for your choices and opportunities, you open yourself to becoming a victim.

At first, being assertive can be scary because you may have a fear of rejection or failure. This fear is a negative emotion. All negative emotions interfere with positive emotions and contribute to the retardation of your wishes for a better life. Remember, negative emotions produce more negative emotions, and positive emotions form the groundwork to create more positive emotions. The more you speak up, the more confidence you will have in yourself, and the more others will accept you. You must learn to make your own decisions, think for yourself, and accept the results. Always be assertive with kindness and a smile. You won't always get what you want, but you will get respect, and you will get more than you ever dreamed possible before you dared to express your thoughts and feelings.

Assertive or Aggressive

Being assertive is not being abusive or aggressive. When you assert yourself with respect, it is powerful and will bring you respectful responses. Assertiveness is not the same as aggressiveness. Aggressiveness can be perceived as hostile or, if enacted in a pleasant, friendly manner, as helpful and respectful. You do not need to express yourself with force. You should speak with assured calmness and politeness. Your thoughts and ideas just need to be communicated with firmness, and with practice, you will become more and more able to do that.

Aggression can be selfishly demanding what you want at the expense of others. It generates anger, hostility, and fear. You may achieve short-term goals, but you lose in the long-term. You lose the friendship, trust, and respect of the people you bully through your aggression. You may keep some of your companions, but they will fear you, and you cannot develop sincere and lasting relationships. When you are assertive, you stand up for your rights and respect the positions of others. It is simply an expression of your feelings and the truth about what you expect or want. It becomes easy to say no once you do it several times. Always be honest about why you tell someone no and do it in a polite, respectful manner. You do not help anyone when you succumb to their demands that you do not want to do. They are using you when they ask you to go out of your way unnecessarily. When you allow people to use you for reasons that make you feel diminished in any manner, you lessen the power of your spiritual essence. As you grow spiritually more robust, you will not allow people to use you unless you do it for a good reason and you want to.

Define for yourself what you will put up with from others—set boundaries for how you will allow them to treat you. Also, define for yourself how you will treat others. When you set standards for yourself regarding what you will tolerate, you give yourself the right to experience positive relationships. You will lose some friends, but they are not your friends if they abuse your friendship. You may tell people how to treat you. Most people will treat you how they perceive you and want them to treat you. Some will abuse you if they feel they can get away with it, so it is up to you to set them straight.

Relax and Tell It Like It Is

When unhappy with the words or actions of others, put yourself in their place. Try to understand why they act as they do. Then you can tell them how you would like them to change course in a friendly way. The secret is always to be respectful but pleasant and firm. The more you do it, the easier it becomes.

Refuse to blame, criticize, or insult the other person to prove you are right. Do not make excuses for yourself. Anything that has ever upset you is in the past, and the future will be different. Many subtle changes and even fast, radical changes will occur. That is good. Say what you feel and mean what you say. You don't have to get your way every time. You can give in or compromise as long as you understand why you are doing so and feel you are doing the right thing for yourself. When you allow someone to abuse you, it is you who allows it. Many people get into a situation where they have an abusive spouse. When they first get married, everything is hunky-dory, wine, and roses. Then things deteriorate for reasons unknown to the abused spouse. The abused person just doesn't know what to do about the situation. They are ashamed to tell anyone about their condition and feel that it is their fault that the abuse is going on. They will typically do everything they can to keep the marriage together until the abuse becomes clear to others. Only then will they attempt to get out of the situation, sometimes with the police's help. However they do it, it is an essential step in developing the internal strength to bring happiness to their life. You cheat yourself when you do nothing to bring joy or satisfaction to your spiritual essence or physical life.

Be clear to others about what you want from them. Please do not be shy about telling them. If you do not stand up for yourself, others will decide to control your life. When that happens, your spiritual growth becomes stagnant. The idea is to have direct, open, honest communication with everyone with whom you associate. The trait of assertiveness will help you control stress and anger and improve your coping skills. Assertiveness is a fundamental communication skill. Assertiveness means you express yourself effectively and stand up for your unique perspective while respecting the beliefs and words of others. It will help you raise your level of self-esteem and earn you the respect of others. Assertiveness is communication based on mutual respect. It shows that you respect the other person's opinion while standing up for your interests and expressing your thoughts and feelings. It shows that you are aware of their rights while being aware of your rights and will work with them to resolve all conflicts. When you are silent or passive, or too aggressive, your message often gets lost. People become too busy thinking about answering you rather than digesting your message.

If you are laid back or tend to be passive, the thought of being assertive may bother you. You might routinely go along with whatever the other person or group you are with dictates. You probably hate conflict and avoid it. When you just go along to get along, you send a message that your thoughts, ideas, and feelings are not as important as those of other people. They make you from the same spiritual energy as they are, so there is no difference in how important, good, or bad, either of you is. It is the same energy just experiencing different activity. Being a nice person often deceives the people you associate with by allowing them to ignore your wants. It encourages them to believe that your thoughts and ideas are not important. But you are important. You are just as important as anyone else in the world. We are all spirits wearing physical coverings, traveling through the universe in search of nirvana.

Speak Your Feelings

Have you ever taken on a project because someone you have a friendly or semi-important relationship with asked you to do it? After you took it on, you realized you did not like doing it or are inept at it? And then you backed out of the job? Accepting the project caused you internal conflict, and then getting out of it was even more stressful. Your stress was your fault. Behavior like this can introduce feelings of victimization, resentment, anger, hopelessness, stress, and inferiority. Your first responsibility is always with yourself. If you ever expect to help others, you must first take care of yourself.

Many passive, shy, and soft-spoken people abused by the pushy behavior of others eventually tire of it and explode. At first, they might express their feelings through sarcasm or complain about their situation to their family or close friends without confronting the person who is the actual cause of the problem. They are uncomfortable expressing their true feelings. Some people eventually just blow up and scream at their antagonists. Angry screaming is not healthy for anyone. Overall, this type of passive-aggressive behavior will harm the relationship, destroy mutual respect, and make it very difficult to associate with each other.

Unhappy and aggressive people may get their point across, but they do not endear themselves to others, and because anger puts pressure on their spiritual essence, that restricts their thought process. It is important to avoid being enraged or violent because it is bullying and often intimidates the recipient. Being assertive with a smile and friendliness instead of being frenetically aggressive is a much more robust and healthier communication style. First, it keeps people from walking all over you. It protects you from bullies and allows you to get your point across. When you learn to be assertive, you grow in confidence and self-esteem. You will like yourself more, and it will improve your physical and mental health. It will also strengthen your spiritual essence. You will learn what it is to receive honesty and respect from others. They will understand what you want and how you feel about it. Your decision-making skills will improve, and your relationships will improve. You will lose friends who have repeatedly taken advantage of you, but you will replace every one of them with a better friend.

Express Truth

We learn to assert ourselves. For example, Ronnie worked on an oil rig when he got out of high school. After about six years of working in the oil fields, he desired some other work, so he quit and got a salesperson job. He did reasonably well at his new job, but his customers occasionally complained to his boss that what they received was not what they expected.

The complaints bothered Ronnie because his customers were important to him, and he wanted them to like him. While talking about the problem with his boss, his boss said, "Just be honest with them." This nonplussed Ronnie. He had always thought he was honest, and no one had ever called him dishonest. He thought it over for some time before he realized, no, he hadn't always been honest. In fact, he had been lying all of his life. Like most people, they had taught him that one must be nice to everyone, and he always tried to be nice to people. He had interpreted that message to mean he shouldn't bother to correct the message when people took the wrong meaning from something he said to them. He was allowing his customers to purchase things from him under false premises. When he realized what he had been doing, he felt horrified and made a vow to be more honest.

Soon, while talking to a customer, he realized the customer thought he would benefit more than he actually would. When Ronnie realized this, he immediately knew he had to tell the truth. He was absolutely shaking when he explained what the benefits were. To Ronnie's surprise, his customer readily accepted his explanation and made the purchase. It got easier to be honest with every sales presentation he made. And low-and-behold! Ronnie's sales increased. His skill as a salesperson snowballed, and within a year, he became his company's top salesperson.

As another example, Abby was always respectful of her husband, but it did not do her much good. He expected her to take care of the children in the morning, get them out of bed, feed them, take them to school and then clean the house and have a hot meal ready for him when he got home from work. If anything was out of place when he got home, he would criticize her for it. If she did not cook the food like his mother used to cook it, she heard about it. He never complimented her and often criticized her. She did her best and did not talk back to him because she felt it was her responsibility to keep him happy. After all, he married her, and she thought she owed it to him. Also, he was the breadwinner, and she felt she had nowhere else to go. After seventeen years of marriage and three children, it finally happened. Abby's dinner was not up to her usual quality, and he told her she needed to learn how to cook.

The way he said it touched a nerve in the back of her brain, and she exploded. She started yelling at him, cursing him, and told him he could cook for himself. Unbelievably, she terrified him. He backed off and told her he was sorry. He changed. She did too. She learned to tell him the truth about her feelings and settle down and speak calmly, directly, and with politeness. The important thing was that she learned to tell the truth about her feelings, and he was intelligent enough to listen to her. The first explosion is often the first step in the breakdown of unhappy marriages that appear happy to outsiders.

And then there was Jerry Spangler, who was unhappy with his life. His family and friends constantly put him down. He had an older brother who criticized everything he did. When he was in high school, his brother would say he must have had an easy teacher if he got good grades. When he played on the high school football team, and the team lost a game, his brother would tell him he was stupid for playing on such a lousy team. His mother constantly worried over anything he got involved in, hoping he wouldn't get hurt or wondering if it was the right thing for him to do. When he got married, his wife and mother would worry about him right in front of him, concerned if he could be successful at his job. He tolerated it for years until he finally got mad and told them how to treat him. He said to them he wanted them to treat him with respect and politeness. He was shaking, and his voice wavered the first time he told his family off. They had verbally abused him for most of his life, so it was close to impossible for him to speak up for himself. But he did, and the first time he did it, everyone looked at him like he was crazy, but his older brother apologized and started treating him with more respect. This minor success encouraged him to speak up to others; some people obliged, others did not. Now he is better off and much happier, and he has many more friends.

As you become assertive, there is one more vital facet about yourself you will learn, and you will love it. You will know who you are. You will recognize how to use your mind to improve every aspect of your life. Your mind is the spiritual aspect of your soul that controls your life on earth.

Thoughts

- Be honest with yourself about your feelings
- Listen to the words and emotions of other
- Speak honestly about your emotions
- You are the creator of your destiny
- Assertiveness can be scary
- Refuse to insult people
- Tell people what you want and expect from them
- Be calm and use your smile when you are assertive
- You may speak your truth

CHAPTER 8

THE MYSTICAL MAGIC OF MIND

While we actively use our bodies while we exist in physical form on earth, we often overlook our most beautiful feature. That is our actual self, our spiritual essence. We are spiritual creatures formed from a universal spiritual nature. What we call our mind is our spiritual essence expressing itself.

You have physical aspects of spirit and invisible elements of spirit. Your mind is spiritual. It is energy at the quantum level. You constantly communicate with nature on the quantum level to determine your life decisions, ideas, and actions. Communication between one's mind and one's soul is a little difficult for some people to understand. Still, our mind is an essential part of our soul. We control our destiny with our soul. With a bit of practice, you can use your mind to improve your spiritual being in every way possible.

Our spiritual essence chooses the thoughts we think. Our dominant thought patterns manifest in our lives. What we think about manifests in our reality. To use our mind's power, we must first accept that we can act on our reasoning. We admit we can have worthwhile and good ideas and that it is our right and duty to work on our visions. Many people hold themselves back, never daring to try anything without begging someone else for permission. Suppose you want to follow through on your ideas. If you believe they are beneficial and come from your desire to improve something, there is no reason, especially someone else's criticism, for you to stop. You have just as much right as anyone else to experience love, joy, and success in your life.

When we think, we use our minds to send messages to the universe. We send spiritual signals to communicate with the spiritual essence, which frees up energy for the thought to manifest in real life. The power of these thought waves is minimal, and therefore most of our thoughts travel for a short distance and turn to other matters. It is just like when you are meditating on a candle, and the picture of a lion chasing a rabbit keeps entering your mind. An ancient story from antiquity states that we send our wishes to the universe, where the gods discuss them. If they believe you deserve them, they grant your wishes. You deserve whatever you earn or achieve.

When we want anything that is outside of our immediate reach, our mind will help us attain it, but we must be highly focused and accurate. We must work with the universe to accomplish our dreams. The scientific community has, over the past two hundred years, touched upon how spirit works. However, they call it anything but spirit. When you genuinely want to develop your spiritual muscle and attain your dreams and goals, you must use your individual spiritual energy to communicate with universal spiritual energy. You must align yourself to the spiritual energy you desire to bring into your life. Remember, everything, matter and nonmatter, is spiritual energy.

You Attract Your Experiences

In the early twentieth century, Albert Einstein wrote that all matter is composed of energy. He noted that all matter changes and everything in the universe is interconnected. Einstein's ideas led to the revelation that everything in the universe is affected by everything else. Scientists began looking into smaller and smaller sizes of matter until they started looking at particles of energy on the quantum level. Quantum is the smallest amount of any physical entity or property involved in any kind of interaction. Quantum field theory is the fundamental idea in physics that describes atoms and the tiniest scales of subatomic particles. It gets down to the spiritual level of energy. An atom, for instance, is defined as the smallest form of matter. However, some people will claim the smallest particle of matter is the electron, quark, or some other tiny, tiny particle. But try to see or touch a quark or an electron. They are not visible and are impossible to feel as they pass through your body. These tiny particles form the basic fabric in, around, and throughout the universe. In this realm, the spiritual realm, our thoughts, desires, intentions, emotions, and feelings instigate the circumstances and activities of our lives. We live in a universe of spirit, and you are an integral entity existing in this spiritual universe.

When two subatomic particles, such as electrons, are paired in quantum theory, they act as a single unit. When one spins to the left, the other spins to the right, they function in unison. If the direction of the spin of one changes, the direction of the spin of the other also instantly changes. These particles can even be thousands of miles apart, and they still act simultaneously. In 1955, a physicist named John S. Bell came up with the theorem that instantaneous change occurs in widely separated systems. What does all this mean when we talk about spirituality? It means that there is an interconnectedness throughout the spiritual universe. When one quantum or spiritual particle communicates with another, transferring information is immediate. There is communication on the spiritual level, and we, as spiritual creatures, experience that communication every moment of our lives. Communication literally transpires on the spiritual level through the energy carried by waves.

The energy of a particle depends on its primary mass, potential energy, and kinetic energy. The energy of a wave depends on its frequency and amplitude. Experiments have shown that just as a particle knows when to change its spin to conform to its twin's spin, wave particles know what kind of experimentation is going on, and they behave accordingly. When the conductor of experiments with wave particles measures motion, the wave particles become waves. If the observer measures location, they immediately become particles. This type of activity is continually going on throughout the universe, your entire spiritual essence, and your physical body.

Scientists who study these tiny particles and view how they communicate with one another merely study a model of what we continually experience each moment of our existence. They claim this is true, whether in spirit or physical form. Our spiritual essence constantly communicates with itself and comprises trillions and trillions of minuscule spiritual particles. It also communicates with spiritual particles near our immediate self and others not so close. Universal spiritual energy is neutral in its desire to help or hinder our wants. When we produce happy thoughts, there is a tendency to bring happiness into our lives. When we think about miserable things, we attract misery to our lives. This activity is called the law of attraction. Many people study it and avidly work to attract good things in their lives. You can attract good things to your life too.

There Is No Such Thing as a Free Lunch

Many people work at attracting good things to their life by visualizing, meditating, dreaming, and other methods, some of which fail. Every technique, even dreaming, is good because, if nothing else, their minds focus on something good for them. The spiritual energy we communicate with is no more intelligent than we are because it is the same spiritual energy. Because this energy is at our level of thought and feeling, we need to be specific when we attempt to raise our sense of well-being. We need to focus on whatever we wish to achieve. Napoleon Hill once said, "Whatever mind can conceive and believe it can achieve. "Napoleon Hill's statement is correct.

The more specific you are when you conceive and believe it, the better your chances are of achieving it. Some people simply pray for whatever they want to come about. Other people meditate and expect what they genuinely desire to happen. Still, others picture themselves as being what they wish for. Most people make a supposedly sincere wish for what they want to happen and then continue to go about their business and hope their desire comes true. These methods will work. Still, to be truly successful, you must use the total of your mental, physical, spiritual, and emotional self. Most people expect God, the Great Pumpkin, or whoever they recognize as their deity to miraculously deliver their wish to them. They expect their wishes to come true with no effort on their part. It does not work that way.

Spiritual energy, like the average human, looks for happiness and beneficial change. When you project your dreams, wishes, and desires to universal spiritual energy, it wants to help you achieve them. And the universe will help you get what you want when you cooperate with it. Your job is to do what you can to become the person ready to receive what you wish. It is best when you appropriately change your behavior to align with whatever role you want to play in life. You will also improve your chances of achieving your wishes when you study whatever you want to become. You do not have to continuously focus your energy on your goal. Still, it is essential to spend some time every day focused on what you wish for.

You might quickly object and say, "That's not spiritual; that's just hard work." It may be hard work, or it may be a delightful journey. People often forget that we are all spiritual creatures walking around in a body composed of our spiritual energy. There is not much difference between existing in human form and existing in spiritual form. Most people decide they want to be something, or receive something, or accomplish something. They meditate on it or pray to receive it once or twice, and when it doesn't quickly happen for them, they give up. They refuse to make the changes that their spiritual energy is begging them to make. They believe they are going to get something for free.

An ancient story tells about how a great king asked his top advisers to bring him the world's most excellent knowledge and wisest information. His advisers searched for years and finally brought him ten thousand books, ten thousand pages long. He took one look at all those books and told them they filled them with too much information and to do a better job. He said no one could ever read that much information. The search for the world's most important knowledge continued for several years, and his advisers kept bringing him shorter and shorter books. It kept going on until finally, his advisers brought him one book with only one page in it. And on that one page, there was only one sentence. And that sentence had less than ten words. The king looked at the sentence and beamed happily as he read the words, "There is no such thing as a free lunch." In every change and every exchange, there is a transfer of energy. That energy exchange may benefit all entities involved, harm all entities, or be neutral. Still, there is a cost in every expenditure of energy. People want that free lunch, but just as there is no free lunch in the physical world, there is no free lunch in the spiritual universe. Some people become disillusioned, others become cynical, and some people feel sorry for themselves. But the people who go about using their spirituality and the universal spiritual force positively often receive tremendous rewards.

Your Soul Controls Your Body

Here is how it works. You have a goal you want to achieve, or you may be sick and want to recover or even get a particular job. It is always the same. Spirit will work with you if you cooperate with spirit. That is the critical factor that most people ignore. You must work with the universal spiritual essence if you want to be successful. You are a spiritual creature. Everything you encounter is an expression of spiritual energy. Your soul hears, feels, and understands every thought you have. If you dwell on a unique desire for a few moments a day for a week or two and then forget about it, it won't get done. When you learn to stick with your thoughts and physically take on the demeanor of who you will become, results are more rapid. It takes time and patience on your part. It is a very workable and effective means of accomplishing your dreams.

When you wish for some improvement for only a few minutes or an hour, and then go about your business complaining and criticizing others, you neutralize your helpful thoughts. And nothing works. Spirit reacts to and acts on every thought you have. Suppose you have a propensity to feel sorry for yourself. In that case, the universe will ensure that you receive energy in your life that will enable you to feel sorry for yourself. If you quickly become irritated and angry, the universe will bring you opportunities that will allow you to lose your temper. In fact, if you take the time to look at your life for a few months or a few years, you see that you habitually have feelings of happiness, sadness, anger, love, or maybe jealousy. Your emotions and behaviors repeat themselves because you learn to act in specific ways when you react to anything.

You are who you are at present because of everything you have done, experienced, and reacted to in your past. When you experience difficult situations in this physical life, similar events will recur until you learn whatever you need to know. How you feel, how you act toward others, and your spiritual reality pull you into situations to encourage you to develop your spiritual maturity. Your maturity is known as karma; what you sow, so shall you reap. As the Bible states, "Do not be deceived: God cannot be mocked. A man reaps what he sows." (Gal 6:7, New International Version).

People change their behavior when they hurt so badly that they must change to keep their sanity. When your life is satisfactory and you want to improve, you must act. You should focus on what you want to become. And then you need to act as if you have already changed. Then spirit will cooperate with you. Look at it this way. Say you have a friend or acquaintance who keeps asking you to do things for them but never cooperates with you or thanks you for your help. You are sick and tired of it. For months, you have been resenting the fact that this person abuses your friendship. Spirit is just like you. It eventually stops working with or for you if you do not cooperate with it. In fact, if they do not convince that you really want or even deserve whatever you wish for, it will not help you achieve it—especially since you also are spirit. Spiritual particles attract other spiritual particles in which they are in tune. You must instigate at least a tiny bit of activity that will help carry you to the state you desire. In the case of having a friend who takes advantage of you, it may be as simple as telling them you don't appreciate it. When you work with spirit, you need to be fully involved and cooperative with it for it to help you.

There are many ways to count on the universal spirit to help you accomplish your goals. You can visualize yourself as you want to be. You can develop a mantra signifying what you want to become. You can write it down on a piece of paper over and over, or you can repeat it to yourself daily. A mantra is a word, statement, or slogan repeated over and over. Although you have a physical body, your soul controls its activities. It is just as if you have an automobile, and as the person driving that car, you control its movements. Your soul, as your mind, controls your body through your thoughts and feelings. Be good to yourself by cooperating with it.

Decide What You Want and Go for It

You improve your spiritual self by making improvements in every area of your life. Improving your ability to give love, accept love, stay healthy and joyful goes along with spiritual progress. Your present physical life is a learning experience. You learn by listening to the words of other people and doing your best to understand exactly what they say. You use your mind to decipher and comprehend their meaning. You then answer them in a manner that shows you know what they said, and you react and respond to that exact subject. You keep your focus on the topic discussed. Then you practice being what you learned.

You learn by studying ideas and subjects that interest you. You learn by listening to your intuition and acting on it to improve its accuracy. Practice what you want to become. Professional athletes practice every day. Musicians, actors, professional salespeople, teachers, and everyone who works at any type of labor continually do it throughout their life. Whatever you want to accomplish in your life, study it, visualize it, and do something about achieving it every day of your life. You are a spiritual being, and you might as well be in charge of the changes that come to you throughout your life.

When you seriously want your spiritual essence to help you bring about a change, there are several things you can do. First, you must think about it until you have a clear picture of what you want. You can write it down or draw pictures of it and describe it as a mantra. When you write your wish down in complete detail, it gives the thought added power. And don't do it just once. When you spend time every day or two writing it down, it is like souping up an old car to turn it into a powerful racing machine. Psychiatrists say that words only make up 7 percent of verbal communication. Your spiritual essence needs to hear or feel your wants repeatedly to get a perfect understanding of what it needs to do to help you. As you write it out and rewrite it, and constantly verbalize it, it becomes clearer to your soul. Your dreams often become expanded, and you end up achieving even more than you originally planned. It is like an unknown power flow from your fingers up through your arms to your brain. And then this power permits you to follow through on your wishes. You must also concentrate on the thought every day, and then you must practice becoming the person who deserves what you want.

You must become the person who can handle what you want before you receive what you want. There are many programs for achieving your goals. They almost always recommend having an action plan, making a list of intermediate goals, and keeping a journal of your activities. It sounds a lot like plain old, practical, physical effort—doesn't it? That's because it is. And when you practice this concept, it can be gratifying for you, and yes, you will grow spiritually. Spiritual growth happens just like when someone joins a band or a sports team. They may get to play, but they probably will not stay with the team unless they practice every day. It isn't easy at first, but after you do it a few times, it becomes second nature. It can become an enriching way of life. You not only pull your dreams toward you, but you change yourself enough so that you are ready to receive whatever good comes to you.

When you want to use a mantra to help you, pick out a word, sound, or short phrase, signifying what you want to achieve. Any word or sound will do. Say you wish to receive a raise where you work. You first draw, preferably on paper or in your mind, a picture of what you will look like when you receive that raise. Then you write out exactly what you will do to earn that raise so that you will know you deserve it when you receive it. Picture everything about how you will act and feel and who you will be because you will experience a change to achieve your goal. Then pick a mantra and use it many times every day. A simple phrase such as *bubble gum* is just fine. Say you want to become a well-known artist. The mantra you choose will mean to you that you are a famous artist. It is an affirmation, and the more you use it, the more it will become embedded in your subconscious. You don't have to, but you can even picture yourself as that well-known artist when you repeat your mantra. You can say it aloud or to yourself. It doesn't matter. You are convincing your spiritual essence, or your spiritual essence is convincing you to do what you need to do to become spiritually stronger.

Change is continually going on in your life, every second of every day. Besides being universal, constantly changing and vibrating, spiritual essence has thought and is tremendously curious. While we spend time on earth, some of us smother our curiosity, and some of us use it to bring new ideas for the world to enjoy. And some of us simply use it to improve our environment. When you develop a picture of your specific purpose for spending a physical life on earth, you automatically develop guidelines for improving your spiritual strength and vitality.

THOUGHTS

- Everything in the universe is spiritual energy
- The universe is one massive, living entity
- Spiritual energy is neutral in its desire to help us
- Happy thoughts attract happiness
- Be specific in pursuing your dreams
- There is no such thing as a free lunch
- Our souls control our bodies
- Your spiritual self reflects your reality
- A mantra is a powerful tool

CHAPTER 9

PURPOSE IN LIFE

People often feel they must be living on earth to accomplish a specific purpose. Most of them do not know what it is and spend a lot of time figuring it out. You are going to spend time on the physical plane whether or not you decide to have a purpose. Only you can choose your goal. You are in charge. It may be something as commonplace as working as a bricklayer or as unusual as being an astronaut. It is your purpose, and only you can decide what it is. Something must spark your recognition of it. It may come to you while you are daydreaming, while you are in a conversation with someone, or even when you are sleeping.

Since you are spiritual energy, you have existed since the beginning of time. You are experiencing this lifetime to work off karma, or you might be here to take a breather on the way to wherever you are going to exist next. You will live in some form for eternity, just like every other aspect of spiritual energy in the universe. During this eternal existence, you will always have feelings, emotions, and the ability to communicate with and receive energy from your surroundings. In every moment of your life, you experience energy and affect energy. In every moment, you have feelings and thoughts. What you do, experience, and think affects your future. When you decide that you have a purpose in your life, whatever you do about it affects your future. If you want to experience any goodness in your future, it makes sense for you to have a purpose that you can define as good, healthy, or rewarding.

Your purpose will be something you like to do or something you feel is worthwhile. It could be an idea you cannot get out of your mind. If you want to improve your future and carry the feelings and wisdom along with you when you transpire into the spiritual realm, find a life purpose. Finding a purpose can be difficult for many people. But it can be easy for some people, like the little girl who decided she wanted to become a doctor when she was six years old because her father was a doctor. He would take her to his office, and she spent lots of time in his waiting room with his patients. She loved being there, and she kept the desire alive until she reached adulthood and became a doctor. It is a little more difficult for people who have no role model to follow.

At some point, many of us question our reason for living and what kind of life we should have. People sometimes search for their purpose for years, never settling down to decide what they should be doing. Most of us give up and live a life of mediocrity, doing whatever comes our way. We become like rowboats floating with no rudders or paddles in the Pacific Ocean. When the waters are calm, everything is fine, but we are in deep trouble when a storm comes along. The purpose is like having paddles and a rudder for that boat. It gives you something to hang on to during the worst storms. Any goal can serve as your purpose if you pursue it. If you want to have a purpose in your life, you need to follow your dreams. Your goal will become whatever you desire to accomplish, or some change you want to make in your life that you believe will make you feel good about yourself and what you are doing.

Look within to Find Your Purpose

Spiritual essence is naturally curious and can communicate and change into different forms of matter. By the time most people reach adulthood, society's pressures have dampened their enthusiasm for pursuing what they spiritually should do. They go to school and get told what to think and what to believe. No one teaches them how to think or encourages them to follow up on their curiosity. Your natural curiosity will often lead you to your life's purpose. When you pursue what excites you or interests you, you develop a sense of self-worth, inner strength, and the possibility of extending your time on earth. You also create inner happiness. You feel good about your current life and what you are doing. The idea of having a long and happy life is the best reason for developing your purpose for living. Having a goal to achieve keeps you motivated, and being motivated keeps you moving toward your goal. This type of movement is healthy for not only your physical body, but also your spiritual and mental self.

If your activities are not in line with your dreams and wishes, it is wise to stop doing what you are doing and pursue your dreams. You think, *"That sounds good, but I have other responsibilities."* Of course you do, but that does not mean they have to be your priorities. Your health, happiness, and well-being need to come first. When you give up, you penalize not only yourself but whoever you want to help because you give up your ability to do a good job. When you make your dreams your priority, you help yourself, and you gain the freedom to become your best self. Still, you also give any person for whom you are sacrificing yourself the opportunity to improve their well-being.

Unfortunately, most people must work hard to discover their purpose. Their childhood conditioning, life experiences, education, relationships, and everyday activities smother it. They become so engaged with their daily living habits that any idea of a personal purpose is just a glimmering, flashing light far off in the distance. They go through life feeling unfulfilled and lacking. But by having a purpose, your attention becomes focused on activities that contribute to your well-being and happiness. It also strengthens your spiritual energy and keeps you in a state of equilibrium, contributing to your good health. You will then carry these happy feelings with you as you enter the next stage of your existence. You can always influence your emotions.

An excellent way to find your unique purpose is to look inside of yourself. It is natural and easy to look around and find something worthwhile to do. It is also easy to look around and see activities that will bring you lots of money or fame. But searching outside of yourself will only tell you what other people are doing. You find your true purpose within your soul. It will be something you really enjoy doing or something that is not enjoyable but that you believe is necessary to do. Your true purpose will always enlighten and be beneficial to someone.

When you look within, you are much more likely to find an inclination to do something submerged in your subconscious. Some people drift along from job to job until they accidentally stumble into something that means the world to them. Stumbling into it is just as good of a way to find a purpose as any other. When someone works to make a living doing something they do not enjoy or at least believe is contributing to society, they will never achieve the spiritual changes they can earn while acting on their purpose.

Your Goals Help You Become an Expression of Your Soul

If no inclination toward your purpose comes to mind, do the first helpful thing that you can do. Your purpose will not be an activity that is selfish but something that is beneficial, in line with your ethical reasoning and something you can actively pursue. Any activity you can get involved in that stops you from focusing on your self-interest will allow you to forget about self-preservation and learn what abilities you have and how you can use them for the greater good. Whatever you get interested in could very well become your purpose in life. When you pursue interests within yourself, it brings you into the present moment and creates a calmness that allows you to listen to your inner voice. And that is the message from which your purpose in life will come.

While you are working to learn your purpose, think about your past successes and failures. Think about the activities you have been involved in when you felt very much in harmony with yourself. The idea is to build on what you already have as a basis to start with. If you haven't accomplished anything or at least feel you haven't, or if you do not want to pursue anything you have already been exposed to, just dream. Imagine yourself figuring out what you would like to be. Spend time viewing yourself as a wonderfully successful person. Then ask yourself what you are good at. Ask yourself what you did to become successful. The idea is to be moving toward a goal. Having a goal to achieve is more important than what the goal is. Start by acting on your dreams. Activity produces more activity, and that is what will lead you to your purpose. When you get involved in a project with a goal, and it is in sync with your interests and ethics, your life will become more exciting and rewarding. The rewards and excitement will be there even if you never achieve your goals.

Setting your goal isn't the end of the journey; it is the beginning of a lifelong journey that will give you a fundamental reason for living. And it can prolong your life. Every day is a brand-new opportunity for you to create the person you need to be. When you pursue your purpose, you gain a whole new meaning for your life on earth. You become happier and enjoy the process while growing inner spiritual strength.

You will learn to appreciate your success

As you become involved in pursuing your purpose, you will notice the needs of others and recognize that whatever you are doing not only makes you feel good but also benefits them. You will become involved in making improvements in your life and the lives of others. You will develop empathy for the suffering of others and work to make their lives better. Even if you are unsuccessful at improving the lives of others, you will learn new skills that benefit you in some way. It is the activity and the intention that help you become more in tune with your spiritual self. As you become more in tune with your spiritual essence, you naturally become happier and healthier.

As you pursue your purpose, it doesn't matter what specific skills you learn or improvements you make. You will develop an understanding of what it means to help other people and yourself. Even if you pursue a purpose and it doesn't work out after a while, it's OK to change your goal or purpose. What matters is that you are enlarging your spiritual understanding of what you need to do to have a joyful and comfortable future in the spiritual realm. You are preparing yourself for the time when your vital spiritual energy separates from your physical being to become a purely spiritual entity.

Along with your pursuit of a purpose for your life, you will lose any propensity you have to be self-centered. You will learn to appreciate the strides you make toward achieving your goals. You will experience genuine gratitude for the help you receive from others, which will be a remarkable contribution to your happiness and self-worth. Whatever you pursue, however successful you are at it, you are going to profit from it, possibly more than anyone you help along the way.

You will become deeply involved in developing your goals and losing any addiction you may have for temporary pleasure. Watching television, visiting with acquaintances just for the sake of having something to do, and spending your time gossiping about others will no longer interest you. You will become focused on what is important to you. In fact, when other people talk negatively about you, you subconsciously realize that they are just describing their own emotions and that whatever they have to say has nothing to do with you. You may respond to them or ignore them, but you will not allow their thoughts to interfere with your joy, desires, or ambitions. You will become an outward expression of your spiritual self.

You Attract What Your Soul Generates

People are like crabs piled up in a large bucket. When one crab starts climbing out of the bucket and gets a little higher than the other crabs, one crab at the bottom of the bucket will reach up and grab the crab that is escaping. It will pull the escaping crab right back down to the bottom of the bucket. This will not happen to you because when others try to pull you down, as they almost certainly will, you will just ignore them and go about your business. Everything changes, from letting go of fear, anger, and procrastination to changing your habits and finding work that matters. Life is whatever *you* want it to be. Don't let anyone decide how you should live your life. A sleeping, spiritual creature lies dormant inside of you, waiting to conquer the world. However, you must take the first step and dare to dive into the unknown. Nobody will ever know how awesome you are if you don't show them.

Plan to make your earth life an enjoyable adventure. There is no need to become stressed about finding your purpose. It may be something wildly complicated and inspiring. It may be as simple as encouraging others and expressing words of love and kindness to everyone you associate with. And please allow yourself to feel joy, love, and happiness. It is not a sin to be happy, and it costs nothing. You attract into your life what you feel and what your spiritual essence is signaling to you. Your soul is like a magnet that pulls similar energy into your being. Think of yourself as an energy transmitter and receiver. You constantly send out signals that tell the universe who you are in this moment and what you want at this moment. Those signals will either attract or repel other spiritual and vibrational feelings, thoughts, beings, events, and experiences. You naturally attract that which is in harmony with your spiritual state of being, and you'll repel that which is out of sync with your state of being.

Never forget that you are here for eternity. Your time on planet Earth is a brief period of your entire existence. Your spiritual self will still exist long after your physical body has ceased to exist. Remember that our time on earth is a training period for our next period of existence. Whether we reincarnate or go to another dimension, we will still exist. Now is the time to learn about feeling good, experiencing happiness, and expressing love in any manner possible. This lifetime is your time to learn. It is crucial to involve yourself in the activities that bring love, joy, and self-confidence into your life. It is also the time for you to learn to express your goodness to others.

There are riots worldwide at this time in history, and people express hate and anger about what they consider as the horrible activities of other people. These rioting people spread their anger and encourage people who see them to express their anger and unhappy thoughts. The emotions are contagious and unaware people quickly pick them up. We can only counter these feelings by generating love, joy, and honesty. If you want to experience love and happiness in your future, you must learn how to share them now.

If your soul radiates wealth and abundance, your physical reality will attract wealth and abundance. If your soul radiates anger and frustration, your physical reality will attract that as well. Since the signals you're sending out at any moment are reasonably complex, your experience of physical reality will be equally complex. Once you can accept that your vibrational self attracts compatible patterns, it becomes clear that you must somehow change the signals you're putting out if you want to experience something different in your life. To put it simply, if you want goodness to come into your life, you must fill your thoughts with goodness not just occasionally, but in a large proportion of the time.

If you want happiness and are unhappy, take a long, deep look at the people you associate with. Are they contributing to your happiness, or is there something that they do that keeps you upset? Also, examine your thoughts and behavior. You deserve to be happy, and you alone can make sure that you are.

THOUGHTS

- Discovering purpose is the beginning of a journey
- Your purpose can give you a reason for living
- It is natural for others to want to hold you back
- Accomplishment produces feelings of self-worth
- Look within yourself to find your purpose
- Your purpose is for you alone to determine
- You don't need to have a purpose
- Always remember you are spirit energy
- You are constantly rehearsing for your future

CHAPTER 10

THE ROAD TO HAPPINESS

The energy surrounding you will both affect and be affected by your energy as you carry feelings and information throughout eternity. Your default emotion may be anywhere between overwhelming love to deep, dark anger. What we feel in our physical life will carry over into our spiritual life. What you experience regarding your happiness is determined by you. The time you spend on earth is an opportunity for you to understand, cooperate with, and improve your spiritual self. You can help yourself enter your next phase of existence between any range of happiness of your choice.

The Merriam-Webster dictionary definition of happy is: "favored by luck or fortune, notably fitting, effective or well-adapted, enjoying or characterized by well-being and contentment, having or marked by an atmosphere of good fellowship, friendly and enthusiastic about something to the point of obsession." All of us start our earthly life as babies with a default level of emotional happiness, sadness, anger, or even melancholy. We bring these emotions with us at birth. Everything we do and experience affects our emotions, and they constantly change, just like all energy in the universe. Most people do not think about the idea that they can improve their level of happiness. They go through life experiencing whatever comes their way.

Earth life gives us many opportunities to develop the level of happiness or unhappiness we want to experience. We have the chance to work, meet many diverse people, get married, and engage in a plethora of other activities. When our physical energy turns to spiritual life, we carry whatever happiness we have obtained on earth right along with us. Suppose you want to experience pleasure throughout eternity. In that case, it helps to use your earthly life to develop the trait of joy. If you believe you should experience unhappiness or hurt during your time as a spiritual entity, feel right at home with being angry, dissatisfied, or unhappy. It appears that many people want to experience negative feelings after they separate from their physical bodies. They do nothing to create happiness for themselves or others during their time on earth.

Happiness Is Emotional and Mental

With some people, the very fact that they long to be happy and acknowledge their dearth of happiness makes their unhappiness that much worse. They focus on the fact that they are unhappy rather than following a plan that helps them create happiness. Some behaviors that lead to unhappiness are worrying about the future and clinging to past painful experiences. Cheerful people tend to live in the present. They recognize that worrying and complaining do nothing but interfere with other more valuable activities. When you worry, complaining, or focusing on anything not pertinent to your happiness, improvement, or success, you are wasting your time. Worry and unhappiness do nothing for the body, mind, and soul but cause unhealthy stress and become habitual thought trends. People who constantly criticize or complain are breeding grounds for unhappiness—their own and that of anyone who associates with them. People who easily get insulted or feel that others abuse them make it easy for themselves to be unhappy. It quickly becomes a habit.

Research shows that cheerful people are more successful and healthier and occupy their physical bodies longer than unhappy people. Cheerful people are more energetic and creative than unhappy people. In fact, angry people often make stupid decisions, which contributes even more to their unhappiness and makes other people feel bad. Some people who are happy with their lives allow contentment to set in and sit back and enjoy the fruits of their labor. When this happens, the momentum of happiness can slow down, and other emotions can arise. The lack of effort to remain happy can allow a change in their satisfaction. When they enter an unhappy environment, they can pick up anger, jealousy, hurt, or other negative emotions.

Hopefully, you want to take happiness, joy, and all that is good with you when you cross over to the spiritual realm. In that case, you must know how to generate happiness within yourself. Many people do not understand what happiness is, how to develop it, or even whether it is possible to realize it during their life on earth. Happiness is a feeling of well-being and pleasure. Happy people feel good about themselves and the happiness of others. It is a feeling of freedom, and there is no feeling of hate or animosity toward anyone or anything. Continual happiness comes when you can adjust to whatever circumstance you find yourself in and keep an attitude of joy. This attitude allows you to learn and change in a way that maintains your positive equilibrium.

When you have a satisfying experience, happiness will percolate throughout your being. It is an emotional and mental state that ranges from peaceful contentment to intense joy and delight, ecstasy, or jubilation. Happiness is fun. It is healthy, and it is good for your physical and mental health. Happy people are more creative and more effective problem solvers than unhappy people are. Cheerful people attract friends quicker and more efficiently than miserable people do. They do better at their work and make faster reversals in the event of adverse circumstances and failure. Being happy is better than being unhappy in every way imaginable. It is puzzling why anyone would choose to be miserable or cause another person to be unhappy.

Make Happiness a Habit

Many people go through life just accepting whatever positive or negative energy enters their life, never thinking about what they need to do to experience happiness. Say you want to have a happy and productive future spiritual existence. In that case, you need to develop that inner happiness while on earth. People often say that you can't build happiness by being happy. They say you have to do something for other people to be happy. Doing stuff for others is only partially true. If you refuse to work at developing the trait of happiness, you might never be satisfied. There are many ways to learn how to be happy and raise your default level of satisfaction. If you ask people if they are happy in their lives, many will respond that they are even if they aren't. Joy is very personal and is a beautiful feeling.

Even people who have a default energy level of happiness are susceptible to being pulled down by adverse events, people, or situations. The road to happiness and the ability to keep a default level of happiness is the responsibility of each soul. It is important to practice being happy during periods of stress or crisis. One of the most common ideas about raising one's happiness level is remembering childhood happiness times. Sometimes this is difficult if you had an unhappy childhood, such as cruel parents or siblings. But there are almost always positive memories one can pull up. Receiving a favorite doll, receiving a present from a special friend, or riding a bicycle may bring up pleasant memories.

Developing the trait of being thankful for what you have is a fantastic way to raise your happiness level. It is called an attitude of gratitude. Gratitude is not an easy trait to develop if you don't have it. Start reviewing everything you own and refuse to take it for granted that it is yours. Start focusing on the things you have rather than the things you don't have. When you do this, you realize that you have stuff that other people don't have. Maybe you walk with a limp, and your legs often hurt. That is not enjoyable. But when you see someone with no legs, you realize you are more fortunate than someone without legs. Some people have never been grateful for anything in their lives. Their parents possibly gave them everything they ever wanted, or maybe they entered this life with an attitude of ungratefulness. You can learn appreciation by consciously focusing on how anything you own has benefited you in some manner. Say you own a car. You use the vehicle to take you to work, go on trips, and buy groceries. Do you enjoy doing these things? Focus on what it would be like if you had no car. Examine what the difference in your life would be. Go deep and mentally and emotionally put yourself in the state of being without. How you would feel if they deprived you of your car. The feeling of deprivation can be difficult to manufacture for many people.

As a typical example, a sixteen-year-old child receives a brand-new car for his birthday. His parents gave him everything he wanted all his life. He accepts the car as something he deserves, not even getting excited about it. He sees it as just another trinket to play with or use until it wears out, and then he can get another one. It is challenging for someone like this to learn the joy of being appreciative.

Everything in life is temporary

Gratitude is a beautiful trait, but often must be learned by reasoning. If a person has never needed to be gracious, there is very little reason for them to develop the quality. When you consciously attempt to be grateful for what you have, such as good health or a loving family, you develop the trait. We supposedly should count our blessings, but how many of us do? When you can look within yourself and feel thankfulness for something, you will have gratitude. It comes when you can discern the difference between having and not having while really feeling it. The more you can understand your good fortune to have something, the more likely you will develop this remarkable trait. It makes no sense to wallow in the negative because all it produces is unhappiness. But it is easier than making a concerted effort actually to be happy.

Happiness and unhappiness are habits. You change habits by changing your viewpoint about what is currently happening in your physical life. Maybe someone you look up to was nice to you one time. That is something about which you can feel good. Maybe, before you hurt your leg, you were a superb dancer. That is also something you can not only be grateful for but also admire about yourself. And you can visualize your leg healing in the future. Having goals to work toward is a harbinger of happiness, and you can be grateful not only that you have a dream, but that you can work to accomplish your goal. The effort you put into achieving your goal also brings good feelings to your physical and spiritual body. These good feelings are what translates as happiness to your spiritual essence.

Another way to raise your default level of happiness is to accept responsibility for all your actions and analyze the things you believe you need. You may realize that many of your so-called needs are wants. When you focus on your responsibilities and how to take care of them, it gives you the energy to handle them properly. As you take care of your responsibilities, good internal vibes build up within you, increasing your happiness quotient. Always take pride in your accomplishments and congratulate yourself for every positive outcome of any action you take. Accept the fact that you are a winner and that you can overcome any barriers. Dare to do your best in every endeavor.

Let's face it. Everyone has days when they do not feel well, or they run into obstacles in their work. A friend lets them down or something frustrates them. The typical reaction is to get angry and strike out at someone or get quiet and fume. To turn this or any other frustrating occasion into a time when you can still feel happiness, you only have to change your perspective about it. First, you can look at it as a learning experience and quiz yourself about what you want to learn from the experience rather than question why it is happening to you. You can also look at the experience as training to overcome more significant challenges. You can accept that you will not have to deal with it anymore after you learn whatever you must learn. Realize that frustration is a normal part of life, and it is not unusual or bad for life to be less than ideal at times. In fact, physical life is all about learning, growing, and becoming a more perfect you. Accept that you are just going through an initiation into your next step to becoming an evolved soul.

Always remember that everything in life is temporary. Decide that you will not allow any passing difficulty to control your mood or anything else about your life. You are the dictator of your fate. There is nothing extraordinary about smiling when everything is lovely. Still, it shows internal strength and enlightenment when you can keep smiling while everything appears to be falling apart. To relax and smile when the world is imploding is true power.

Simple Kindness Helps

Everyone's path to happiness is different, but the challenges we face while in our physical bodies allow us to learn how to be happy or, if we so choose, to be unhappy. Everyone goes through times of stress and difficulty. It is how we respond to these times that allows us to build the inner strength to relax and calmly and happily survive tough times. The relationships we have with other people from the second of conception to the end of our physical lives have a powerful influence on our happiness. People who have solid, close relationships with their family and friends tend to live longer than unhappy people. They have happier, healthier, and more robust defense systems against stress and unexpected disasters. They are survivors. They have strong self-worth feelings and have more people they can count on than their less happy contemporaries.

When you can experience happiness regularly, it increases your ability to adapt to new experiences. It helps you steadily improve your every act and thought. You will be realistic about the good and not-so-good that enters your life. Still, you will also be able to focus on the positive possibilities that can arise out of any situation. Happiness is a way of life. It is a critical component of your preparation for your future existence.

Your every thought and action imprints itself on your spiritual essence. Cheerful people focus on what they have and are grateful. Unhappy people dwell on what they don't have, how poorly they are treated, and how unfair life is. There is a stark contrast. It is not only good to practice the art of happiness; it is mandatory if one wants to carry the feelings with them into their future existence.

If you haven't yet developed the habit of happiness, it is time to start. It is an important quality you can carry with you when your spiritual energy separates from your physical energy and carries you into the amazing time of a potentially wonderful existence. Men who enjoy art, ballet, and other cultural activities feel happier and healthier, according to a May 2011 study published in the *Journal of Epidemiology*. The result held even after researchers controlled for other happiness-influencing factors, such as income. For men, physical activity, outdoor hobbies, and volunteer work are also linked with happiness. The cheeriest women attended both church and sporting events. Cause and effect aren't certain (maybe happier people take in more culture than the other way around), but the message is clear: it can't hurt to get out there and do something.

If you're happy, and you know it, what's your secret? Researchers have uncovered plenty of factors, from genes to personal characteristics to life choices, that seem to coincide with happiness and well-being. Here are a few you might have some control over. Are you a curious person? Science has shown that curiosity is a common trait of happy people. In fact, the lack of curiosity is a harbinger of depression. Act on your curiosity. Your spiritual essence is naturally curious, as is all spiritual energy. When you are in your totally spiritual phase of existence, your curiosity will lead you on an ever-changing hunt for adventure. In fact, we can classify your time on earth as an adventure.

Be an example for others

Pets are a major source of happiness. Pet owners enjoy feelings of love, joy, happiness, and strong self-esteem when caring for their animals. The old-fashioned power of positive thinking helps develop the happiness trait. People who write two or three good things that happened to them every week tend to have a high happiness level. This happiness habit produces a whole distinct reality than what the average person experiences.

The habit of thanking people for their kindness to you and the ability to experience gratefulness for things you receive or share also gives rise to your ability to experience a high level of happiness. Hugs, physical affection, and warm embraces with someone you love are strongly related to happy relationships and life. People who volunteer for charities in the spirit of helping others tend to live longer. They even linked altruism to stronger relationships. A recent study found that the most charitable people were likely to have happy marriages. People who give to charity tend to be pleased about it and their lives.

Happiness is not only a feeling; it is a state of mind that we can create with positive emotions and gratitude. Another way to create happiness is to practice feeling happy. Some people carry unhappiness with them wherever they go. Some people will tell you they don't want to be happy because "every time I get happy, something always comes along and destroys it." There is not much you can do to help that type of person except maybe leave them behind, recommend that they get some counseling, or just ignore them. Each of us must make our own decisions about how we want to spend our lives, and sometimes the best you can do is to be an excellent example for others.

Feelings of Happiness Elevate Your Self-Worth

My friend Stuart lived in a miserable situation. The people he worked with complained constantly, and his family wasn't nice to him. He had very few friends who were friendly to him or treated him with respect. Stuart thought about his situation for several years. Eventually, he concluded he needed to start over some place else. He quit his job, filed for divorce from his wife, and moved to a different city where he didn't know anyone. He felt discouraged and didn't know what to do next. The first thing he did was find a place to live on what little money he took out of his now extinct marriage. He began looking for work and got a job in sales that only paid him a commission when he made a sale.

In the beginning, Stuart was not a very successful salesperson and lived paycheck to paycheck. For two years, he continued to live this way while occasionally being threatened with eviction. Finally, one day, the sales increased with regularity. As his sales improved, his newfound friends treated him with respect and courtesy. His success added a great deal to his state of happiness. The people he worked with promoted him, and he realized he was actually living a decent life. It was as if his newfound success and happiness made his friends happy, too.

Stuart did several things that led to his happier and more successful life. After he left his family, the new people didn't treat him any better than the people he left. After a few months, he examined himself because he thought maybe he was partially responsible for his unhappiness. He decided to be friendly and polite to everyone he met. He also started jumping around his house every day and repeating to himself, "I am happy, I am happy," over and over. He said the words to himself and out loud, depending on how he felt. Stuart enjoyed doing this, and it seemed to help. He studied happiness to find out what it was, and he found out that it was a good feeling throughout his body. And he found he was happy when he was good to other people and when he treated them how he wanted people to treat him. At first, he could not experience happy feelings for more than a few minutes at a time, but the more he worked at it, the easier it became. He worked hard and now his days are filled with pleasure and he is very successful. He still has times when unhappiness enters his life. Still, he bounces right back by reversing his unhappy thoughts, figuring out what he can learn from the situation, and doing whatever he can to improve it. He also spends a few moments every morning reviewing a few things for which he can be grateful.

You handle your own happiness. The feeling of joy elevates your sense of self-worth. It radiates to other spiritual entities in your vicinity. It can be a major part of what you take with you when your soul departs from the physical body. Your time on earth is a training period for whatever you will become and wherever you will go in your next period of existence. At the time of separation, your spiritual cells can travel to many wonderful and exotic places.

THOUGHTS

- Your state of happiness is up to you
- Life gives you the opportunity to learn happiness
- Whining and complaining create unhappiness
- Develop an attitude of gratitude
- Make happiness a habit
- Treat others as you want them to treat you
- Happiness is a feeling and a state of mind
- Life isn't always easy, but happiness helps

CHAPTER 11

THE OTHER SIDE

You were alive before you were alive. Anything that is not living cannot produce something that is living or something that will live in the future. Your adventure here on earth started when one person's living seed combined with another person's living egg. Many people cannot realize this because society only treats healthy, breathing people as being alive. Few people take the time to understand that every part of the living human body is spiritual energy. It is invisible spiritual life massed into one physical-appearing body. They just see the human body like skin and bones covering many organs and other miscellaneous parts.

After the egg and the seed combine, the combination feeds off the mother's energy until it becomes a fully functional child. All the substances that formed the child's matter have been alive since the dawn of the universe. Sometimes the child has memories of past experiences, and sometimes the child doesn't. The child has a predisposition to have certain feelings, emotions, and health conditions from its time spent in a purely spiritual form. While existing on earth in human form and while existing in spiritual form, every spiritual particle of the now living human continually goes through a change process. It brings with it periods of trauma, anger, grief, love, joy, and happiness.

As the child grows and matures, he or she will develop strength, the ability to decide, the ability to think coherently, and the ability to move. This child and the adult version of this child contain billions and trillions of cells. They gain new cells with every breath, with every bite of food, and from other people. Everyone also radiates energy from his or her body. Our auras are constantly spreading tiny bits of living energy that others can pick up. This energy can be positive, negative, or neutral. The energy our auras have affects everything with which it comes into contact. Much like the spread of disease, the energy from our aura can permeate the life of whomever or whatever we encounter.

You get what you deserve

All people are born with the ability to think and make decisions, but do not synchronize these skills until they develop the capacity to learn and move independently. As we grow older, we exhibit the type of behavior that is rewarding to us. Most children who receive a lot of love grow up able to express love. While we are children, we make decisions about how we want to treat others and how we want others to treat us. Some abused children develop a mindset that invites people to treat them poorly. They habitually practice behavior patterns that continue to encourage abuse throughout their lives. Some children who are treated poorly, consciously, or unconsciously, decide to treat others with love and respect. They turn the corner from being ill-treated to being treated well. Other people treated with love as children consciously or unconsciously decide to take advantage of others or treat them poorly. They probably brought a predisposition for their behavior with them from before they began their life on earth.

Upon the end of your physical life, a massive amount of spiritual energy will separate from your body. This energy is you, the honest you, or your soul. At this time, it tends to move toward compatible spiritual energy or become entangled with a different spiritual energy that continues to vibrate and move constantly. The energy that leaves your body still has the same emotions, memories, and intelligence it had when vibrating within your physical body. It is your soul. Just because it has experienced a location change is no reason to lose any of its attributes. Spiritual energy often scatters upon transition and may or may not disseminate and join with similar cells. Each spiritual cell can go on a journey throughout the universe or stick around close to your physical body. They have no control over where they will go. The tendency is for the spiritual essence to maintain a close relationship and be attracted to the energy of similar wavelengths. Your trillions and trillions of individual cells each have the abilities of sensing, thinking, and communicating, just as you do as a fully functional person. When they return to the spiritual reality, they take with them their earthly experiences. Their time on earth allows them to experience an intensity of feeling and expression stronger than what they experience in purely spiritual form. Like attracts like, so the probability is that each cell will find other cells with similar energy. But just as in physical life, occasionally hurtful cells join happy cells, which creates trauma.

Upon your physical death, your soul leaves your body. It will join with similar energy, which will allow you to continue your journey as you were evolving on earth or reach a state of Nirvana. If you have been destructive to yourself or others during your life on earth, you will continue to exist in a place where you can learn to overcome this type of behavior. If you have been the type of person who does not work at bettering yourself on earth, you will land in a spot where you can work to better yourself.

Reincarnation

The ideas about heaven and hell come to us from cell memory when our energies existed in the spiritual realm. Cell memory can bring memories of love, joy, and hate. Just as in physical life, memories may or may not be correct. Fortunate people tend to have happy memories, and unhappy people, the opposite. Some cell memory is about heaven or nirvana or purgatory or hell. Nirvana is an existence filled with love and joy. It is a happy vibration, like a dream world filled with happiness and lots of joyful, loving vibrations. Unhappy energy may go to solid, physical places that restrict the energy's positive vibrations and possibly remembered as the abyss, hadies, or hell.

Many living people have memories of past lives. Those memories are from the cells that contribute to their present physical life and are not necessarily from one past life. They are from whatever the spiritual cells experienced in the past and may not be accurate, just as an adult memory may not be accurate about childhood experiences. An example is someone who remembers their childhood home as being huge. When they revisit it forty years later, they're surprised at how small it was.

You have experienced happy and loving spiritual existences and mean hurtful existences. Your spiritual energy has been here forever. It is precisely the same age as the universe, which can keep you from looking down on so-called evil people or people who have been cruel to you when you think about it. When you clearly understand that you are composed of the same energy as everything in the universe, it becomes easy to figure out that you are no better or worse than anyone else. If a bad person can become good and a good person can turn into a dirty, rotten thug, so can you.

You constantly pass some of your energy back to the universe. When your physical body quits functioning, your soul immediately departs. Still, there is a great deal of energy that remains until your flesh and bone deteriorate and vanish. This energy is part of your spiritual or soul energy. Still, it takes longer to leave your physical body than the other physical and spiritual energy. As you pass from your earthly existence, you will have some healthy, joyful energy and some unhealthy energy that has changed from trauma caused by the vagaries of time.

Just as we have memories of heaven and hell, people occasionally have cell memories of past lives. These memories can be imaginary, inaccurate, or close to actual reality. In some cultures, it is common to have memories of past life, and in others, it is rare. A very intriguing story of reincarnation is the story of a pair of twin girls. Gillian and Jennifer were born on October 4, 1938. Seventeen months before they were born, their parents had two young daughters, aged eleven and six, killed in a horrible automobile accident. When the twins were born, their father felt they were the reincarnation of his two daughters. His wife wasn't so sure, but she was open-minded about the possibility. When the twins began to talk, the possibility of reincarnation became very real to the parents. Knowing nothing about their older sisters, the little girls would ask for the same toys that the deceased girls had played with. These were toys they could not have known existed because the parents stored them after their older sisters' deaths.

The family moved away from the town they lived in before the twins were born. When they were four years old, their parents took a vacation back to the area of their former home. While there, the young girls pointed out places their sisters frequented and told their parents specific details about the accident that killed them. As the girls grew older, the memories of their previous lives gradually disappeared. Still, in her early twenties, one of the girls had a series of visions of herself playing in a sandbox near a garden and an orchard. The parents recognized it as the area where they lived with the deceased older daughter before the younger sister was born. Her memories were very accurate for the person who lived the previous life. This case was unusual because, just as memories fade in your present-day life, memories also fade when you transition to life in the spiritual realm and back again.

Christians generally believe in heaven and hell

There are many stories about deceased people who experienced reincarnation. There are also stories about people regaining brain function after being brain-dead and coming back to life. There are medically supervised studies of near-death experiences where people who have been clinically dead for almost twenty minutes get brought back to life. Scientists used a controversial process on close to one thousand volunteers in one of these studies. It necessitated a complex mixture of drugs, including epinephrine and dimethyltryptamine, designed to protect the body from damage. Although there are some slight variations from one individual to another, all the subjects have some memories of their clinical death period, and most of them described similar sensations. Shared memories include a feeling of serenity, security, warmth, detachment from the body and the presence of an overwhelming light.

The idea of religion also stems from cell memory. The concepts of heaven and hell come from the remembered suffering or pleasure that the original religious organizers had. Throughout history, people have believed in a spiritual afterlife. This is generally a belief that humanity has a spiritual component, the soul, that survives the physical human body's so-called death. Along with reincarnation and spiritual memories, many religions believe in a spiritual afterlife. They almost unanimously think that your physical body dies when you die, rather than slowly transposing back into a purely spiritual energy form. They believe your soul travels to heaven, hell, purgatory, or limbo, a holding place. Most religions have no information about your spiritual self or your soul before you are born or before it enters the human body.

Christians generally believe in a heaven and a hell. Heaven is fantastic, and hell is forever and horrible. Roman Catholics and some other Christian religions also believe in purgatory and limbo. Purgatory is a place you go to work off the karma you receive from your mistakes or sins while living in human form. Limbo is a place for those who die in original sin without being baptized. Buddhists believe that after you stop living in your physical body, you reincarnate over and over until you reach a state of nirvana. At the time of nirvana, there is nothing left. The soul disintegrates, and there is nothing left that can experience pain.

Judaism primarily focuses on life on earth rather than what happens after the soul leaves the physical body, but some Jewish people believe in reincarnation. Other Jewish people believe that evil people simply die, and their souls get destroyed at the time of death. Many Muslims believe the soul slumbers until judgment day, when Allah judges the living and dead. They also think non-Muslims can only reach heaven after spending time in a place of purification. Most belief systems generally state that you go to a good or an awful place when you physically die. The good place usually is a happy place, and an awful place is an unhappy place. Some people who are not religious believe that your consciousness ceases to exist.

Your present life sets the stage for your future

True spiritualism is not a religion, although there are religions that profess to practice spiritualism and even have the word *spiritualism* in their title. Much like most religions, spiritualism is based on the belief that the spirits of the dead exist and continue to live after physical death. Many spiritualists believe that their etheric or spirit body (a duplicate of our physical body) continues to exist along with all memories and one's character after crossing over. When they cross over, they go to a place that accommodates people with similar characters. Good people go to good places, and bad people go to bad, unhappy places. A significant tenet of spiritualism is that spirits can communicate with those still living in many ways, including mentally, physically, and direct voice. People use Ouija boards and conduct seances and psychic readings (commonly called fortune-telling) to get in touch with spiritual entities. They also believe in accepting responsibility for their actions and the idea that the Mind, commonly called God, governs the universe. Some spiritualists organize themselves into churches and have regular meetings.

As soon as you form as a zygote (a fertilized egg) you immediately begin accumulating spiritual energy that enables you to survive as a human being. Throughout your life, you continue to collect and shed spiritual energy. Each particle of spiritual energy you attain has a minimal positive or negative effect on you. This collection and shedding happens throughout life. Your memory becomes distorted when you go through the release from your physical body. Just as when you are born, your cell memory experiences trauma and tends to become disrupted. But your existence is the same.

We have only known for less than two hundred years that everything in the universe is energy, and that energy continually vibrates and is nonperishable and eternal. Universal energy has wonderful traits because it forms every bit of matter and every other phenomenon in the universe. When energy leaves our physical bodies, the process is like, although the opposite of, when we first develop our bodies. It can happen quick or take many years as we continually take on energy and lose energy every second of our earthly lives.

People occasionally get a glimpse of the spiritual state of existence in their dreams, daydreams, or meditations. The spiritual existence is like the physical one, but the feelings are not as powerful as those in our physical body. When in spiritual form, the ability to communicate improves, curiosity is strongly developed, and the number of worlds in which one can exist is innumerable. Every spiritual cell, angel, or soul in the universe has more power than the world's most giant computers. Each cell is constantly seeking ecstasy or what it perceives to be a more rewarding existence. But each spiritual cell is no more intelligent than the average earth creature. What each person does during their earth life sets the stage for their next phase of existence.

You Determine Your Future

Thousands of years ago, Hermeticism, a religious, philosophical, and esoteric tradition based on the supposed writings of Hermes, gave birth to the idea that the universe is a giant brain or mind. In fact, when you look at a picture of a human brain cell, it looks like the atomic network of the physical universe. A Nobel Prize was awarded to two scientists (Chin Ning and Tsung-Dao) in 1957, who proved that subatomic particles have intelligence, which is said to verify that the universe is intelligent. Many physicists believe the universe may be a giant brain because it looks and behaves like one. People on the spiritual path have many beliefs, although this Hermetic teaching ties in closely to the thinking of the average spiritual thinker. The opinion boils down to the fact that the universe is God or the mind of God and everything in the universe comes from the very fabric of God, or the universe, whichever way you view it. There is no separation. We are all united as tiny individual parts composed of trillions of even tinier parts of this beautiful brain/universe.

People have for years placed their spiritual path in the hands of various religions, which usually have strict rules, such as the Ten Commandments. They are a set of rules that give no leeway for changing times and cultural and moral patterns. However, spiritual people believe that while we are still living in physical form, we need to help our soul develop to give it the strength to feel happiness and love or whatever one wants when they return to a purely spiritual existence. Both paths are good, and information about the spiritual way needs to be explained to more people to be better understood.

Our spiritual life is a continuum. When we transpire, we go to an environment for which we have prepared all our lives. People who have led positive, loving, and happy lives and believe in God and heaven will go to the heaven of their belief. People who have been cruel and destructive most of their lives will go to a brutal and destructive environment. The universe is so huge that there are multitudes of environments to which our spiritual essence can go. Deep within you, your spiritual essence will cause your energy to gravitate toward an environment or reality that resembles your present state of existence. You will pursue a state of existence similar to your current state to learn any lessons you did not learn during your stay on earth. You could have a long-term, purely spiritual presence, a short term spiritual existence, or immediately return to earth for more activity in the physical realm. The opportunities are endless. You could go to a futurized Land of Oz, a beautiful paradise, or even an enormous world full of fire and huge rocks. Everything is possible, and you determine what it is by your thoughts and actions while on earth. That is a good reason for you to plan on what you need to do to get to wherever you want to go.

THOUGHTS

- Life is a continuum—forever
- People do what is rewarding for them
- You separate from your body at your so-called death
- There is a possibility of reincarnation
- You will experience many situations throughout eternity
- Thought and knowledge are universal
- The universe may be one humongous thought field
- Spiritual study is not religion study
- You determine your future

CHAPTER 12

THE SPIRITUAL PATH TO NIRVANA

Since the first days that humanoids roamed the earth, people have felt an inner sense of spirituality. The very first people had memories of other places where they had existed. They remembered happy places such as heaven, nirvana, and paradise, to unhappy places like hell, limbo, and purgatory. These memories probably came from cell memory. Science has not advanced to where this information is provable. Still, science has advanced enough to understand that when people transition to a deceased state for a short period and then return to life, they can retain their memory.

Since the beginning of life on earth, our earliest ancestors practiced spiritual ceremonies after the expiration of the physical body's movement, which is called death. At first, single-family groups disposed of the body of the departed one. As tribes formed, the ceremonies grew more extensive. They started the practice of asking the god or gods for help and thanking them for their kindness and support. Many tribes even performed animal and human sacrifices to pay tribute to their gods.

After several hundred thousand years, practices such as Hinduism, Buddhism, and Judaism developed. In Hinduism, the student learns to seek truth in multiple places. Buddhists know that our essential nature is not confined but within us and in everything. In Buddhism, the student understands that after death, one is reincarnated or, if enlightened, achieves nirvana. In Judaism, the student learns one God is watching over us. Seventeen hundred years ago, Christianity, which honors Jesus Christ, began. Since then, thousands of religions have evolved with many rules and laws that they claim we must follow to go to heaven and be with God. With the advance of science, people began to question churches' dogmas but still had deep spiritual yearnings. People always perceive religion as beneficial, but many question its value today.

Each religion declares that it teaches the absolute truth. Many churches teach stories, such as a man living inside of a whale for three days. Some people believe the truth of this story. Still, most people, even those who attend church, consider such a report is pure fabrication. One of humanity's fascinating features is that, as physical beings, we can believe anything we want to believe. Many churches make it their duty to judge certain people as evil and punish them or pray for them. They preach to love everyone but hate the bad guys. Concepts about whom to love and who to hate can be confusing too many. They also teach fear, in that you must obey the laws of the church, or you will go to hell—or maybe purgatory if you are just a little bit bad. Many religious laws can be confusing, such as the commandment, "Thou shalt not kill." In fact, there have been more than one hundred wars fought in defense of religion over the years. It is OK to go to war against people you don't like, but it is a sin to kill anyone. The concept that it is okay to go to war but wrong to kill can confuse people. When you are at war, especially if it is a war where the two sides are using powerful weapons, they will kill many people. It is the teaching of concepts like this that hurts the integrity of religion. But many religious people proudly serve in wars to protect their country. Even when their country is the aggressor, they are still proudly and willingly ready to fight and kill the other side.

People Now Question the Authority of Churches

The commandment to honor thy father and mother sounds forthright and reasonable. But what if your mother beats you with a club every day? It would be difficult to honor someone who constantly beats you. Often, like most of the other rules, this law is rationalized to honor only certain parents. Still, it can cause a great deal of guilt for anyone whose parents abused them. It can also be very harmful to the person who only stays around an abusive parent because of their religious beliefs. They must pay homage to their parents because the rules say they must if they want to go to heaven.

In the past few years, megachurches have evolved. They have weekly meetings with thousands of people in attendance. They listen to inspiring music and a sermon about their church's wonders and the importance of raising money to save the people who have beliefs different from their specific church or religious denomination. The ministers of these churches often become very wealthy. The funds raised to help the poor and the nonbelievers never seem to solve the problem. There always is a need for more money, no matter how wealthy the churches get.

Belonging to a religious organization is very helpful for millions of people. But some church services are merely jazzed-up social functions. The people congregate in a large building and spend an hour or several hours listening to the preacher talk about sin, and they pray together. Then, they have a social period before they break away, only to come back the next week to repeat the same ceremony with different words. They may even have Bible study sessions or Koran reading. The congregation learns about history and sinning and how you must pray to God or god to get to the Promised Land. They preach a lot about what you must not do but teach very little about what is wise to do, except to pray to their God to forgive them for their sins or to take pity on them and give them a free pass to their heaven.

Some religions preach all you must do is meditate two or three times a day and repeat the name of a certain God over and over in your meditations and you will ascend to nirvana. For less than two hundred years, we have known that everything in the universe is energy, and that energy continually vibrates and is nonperishable and eternal. The first humanoids seemed to realize this, as it was the basis for their ancient ceremonies. As the different religions flourished, they developed rules for their followers to obey. People are now beginning to question the authority of the various churches and the laws they enforce. Some people have always accepted that we are all spiritual beings, but now more and more people accept this as the truth. They are looking within themselves for a connection with God or a spiritual universe. The words of the religious teachers ring hollow to them. They believe there must be something more worthwhile than praying to Allah or listening to similar sermons week after week.

We Are Spiritual Beings

We can call these spiritually oriented people the new spiritualists. Spiritualism is already a known religion with a dubious reputation because many spiritualist sects give psychic readings, have seances, and read tarot cards. They often have a leader who does channeling, which means they pass along messages from the spirit world to their followers. This type of spiritual study is not popular and appears to be slowly disappearing.

People have a longing and need to get in touch with their spiritual feelings. Often, these feelings arise from hurt, loneliness, or a feeling that something is missing from, or not right with their lives. These people usually start by attending church services, and many of them end up staying right there. The spiritual setting satisfies their spiritual yearning. They often feel that they have a peaceful feeling when they sit inside a church. But many of these people eventually grow dissatisfied with their religious setting. They reject the teachings or feel they are attending a meaningless social function with no relationship to spirituality. Then they often form small groups to talk about spirituality and their need to develop it. They might have experience with tarot card readers, psychic channelers, and healers in this process. Some will continue along this path. Others will continue to study, inquire about, and dig deeper into how they can satisfy this deep spiritual urge.

Spiritual completeness is an individual path because every person has different needs. The spiritual way differs from the religious route. It does not set down definite rules to follow. That is why it is difficult for many people to get involved with it. There are no hard and fast rules, but there are general guidelines you can follow that will help anyone find their spiritual reality. These guidelines help them achieve joy and inner peace. We discuss the general concepts in the following chapter.

Life is a continuum. We are always learning and forgetting. We are always getting better and sliding backward. The idea is to advance in every period of existence. Our present life is like a game that children play. There is a game called dodge ball where one team of players stands in a circle surrounding the other team players. The players on the outside circle throw a ball at the players inside the ring. When a player on the inside of the ring gets hit by the ball, they must leave the circle. They are out. Some players like running around and dodging the ball. The activity is exciting for them. They like their feelings when they are running around and doing their best not to get hit by the ball thrown at them. Other players do not enjoy the game and would just as soon not play. Sometimes when the ball hits a player, it hurts, and other times, it doesn't sting at all. That is like life. We have good times and not-so-good times, but it is a time for us to make a tremendous advance toward the nirvana or heaven we all aspire to attain.

We are spiritual beings, and while we spend time on earth, we can deal with the same situations as when we cross over to the purely spiritual plane. At any time, we can receive information that encourages us to feel good, happy, and peaceful or causes us to hurt in the deepest recesses of our hearts. Our time on earth is a training period for us to learn how to overcome negative energy. It is a time for us to build up our spiritual strength to allow us to enter our future with self-confidence. While living, learn how to generate feelings of love, happiness, and develop the ability to determine your future course of existence. We know we are best off avoiding those who would willingly harm us. But we often fall prey to those who claim they will help us, and when we accept their help, they take advantage of our goodwill. We must learn how to act with love and joy while affirming our best intentions to improve the environment in which we live.

This Life Is for Training for a Better Future

The spiritual path differs from the religious path. The religious way has rules to follow, while the spiritual path has qualities to develop. Some people choose the religious path, and others prefer the spiritual path. It is up to each individual to decide which way to follow. The truly spiritual person will recognize that we are on planet Earth to learn to exist in a joyful environment filled with love, good health, and wisdom. The truly spiritual person will understand that life on earth is a training period for what is to occur in the future. Instead of going to church, though many will go to church, they work to improve their quality of life so that they can take the wisdom and good feeling along to their next existence.

If you are spiritual, remember to start every day with a goal, a smile, and determination to achieve peace or happiness. There is more to it than just acting happy. To improve your quality of life takes effort. But you can do it, and just by being exposed to the type of information in this book, you will make headway toward achieving your most cherished dreams.

You absolutely can learn to enjoy life and be ready to enter your next existence filled with joy, love, harmony, and wisdom. You deserve to live a life of supreme confidence and physical health. You deserve to receive every good thing that comes into your life. It boils down to you learning the proper ways to feel and behave in this lifetime.

Your life is like a sports team's training time to learn its craft before it plays with other teams. The sports teams compete with one another, but you are only in competition with yourself. Are you improving or sliding back? You want to improve throughout your whole life. Some days you will make small advances, and some days you will make large ones. It is the same with months and years. Some people will encourage you on your spiritual growth, and some will be less encouraging or even discouraging. But when you understand what you need to do to improve your life, you have the fundamentals of spiritual growth, and all you must do is adapt them to your life. You absolutely can learn to attract love and respect into your life. No matter how good you think your life is right now, you can improve your life by developing spiritually solid traits. And you will be wonderfully well-prepared for your next phase of eternity.

There are no hard and fast rules for anyone who wants to live a spiritual life. Still, there are commonsense guidelines that one can use to develop prosperity, happiness, and a powerful feeling of self-worth. These guidelines will reasonably prepare anyone for their next existence wherever it is.

THOUGHTS

- Spiritual ceremonies have been with us forever
- With the rise of science, people began to question religion
- People long to get in touch with their spiritual self
- People look within to find a connection with spirituality
- There are thousands of different religions
- Religion is beneficial for many people
- The path to nirvana is an individual one
- Everyone has times of growth and times of regression
- If it is to be, it is up to me

CHAPTER 13

PREPARE FOR YOUR SPIRITUAL FUTURE

Hopefully, you want to exist in a happy, loving environment during your future as a pure spirit. In that case, you must prepare for it while residing on earth. There are many areas of life on which spiritual people focus.

Meditation

Meditation is the most basic and commonly recognized technique to improve one's spiritual reality. It is easy to understand and simple to do. You can meditate by sitting in a relaxed position, closing your eyes, and repeating a mantra such as *aum* or *ram* or even *shiram*. It is normal to do this at least once a day for about twenty minutes. You can use any relaxing sound you want as long as it has no meaning—willy-willy bang bang, pama-pama boom-boom, or any word or phrase you want. *Ohm* and *shirem* are common ones. They all work. Christian praying can be a meditation. When the Roman Catholics say the rosary, repeating a prayer repeatedly, it becomes a meditation. Long-distance runners easily fall into a meditative state running. People often gather, and one person will lead a guided meditation similar to listening to a hypnotic session. There are all kinds of meditations, and they should always be relaxing.

You can learn to meditate from other people, but never let anyone tell you anything about meditation that might intimidate you. It is easy, and anyone can do it. It is different for everyone. Whatever you get out of meditation belongs to you, and no one can meditate better or worse than you do. You can find information about meditating on the internet, in books, and in many other places.

Shadow Work

Shadow work is essential for progress. To grow spiritually, you must overcome negative issues in your life that hold you back. Many religions also have something similar. As an example, Catholicism has confession and Scientology has clearing. For spiritual people, this is the process of going deep within their minds and digging out every negative thing in their life that might bring unhappiness. The memories can range from past child abuse to current addictions, self-sabotage, and limiting beliefs. You can do this by yourself during your meditations, focusing on memories, or with the help of another individual. Shadow work is challenging, but extremely rewarding.

Aura or Reiki Healing

Recognize your aura. Do exercises to strengthen your aura and recognize the thought that your aura is an extension of your soul. You can see your aura by holding your hand out in front of you, spreading your fingers and looking at the space between and above your fingers. You can also use your aura to create spiritual healing for yourself and others. It is simply the act of lightly laying hands on or slightly above parts of your physical body that are sore or damaged.

Aura healing is a technique of using your hands to transfer spiritual energy between yourself and another person to promote healing. Reiki healing is an advanced form of simple aura healing that teaches how and where to place your hands during the healing. It is taught by Reiki Masters and comes with a set of ethics. Reiki ideals aim to help people consciously improve themselves as a necessary part of the Reiki healing experience.

Curiosity

Embrace your curiosity. It is essential for the development of your spiritual essence. "Little boys should be seen and not heard. Curiosity killed the cat. Mind your own business." By the time most people enter their teenage years, their natural curiosity has been diminished to the point that they just accept whatever shows up in their life. Their lack of interest makes it easier for their teachers and elders because they don't have to explain everything to them. But curiosity is natural for spiritual energy, and you are an outstanding sparkle of pure energy. If no one were ever curious, the significant buildings, highways, ships, rockets, and everything else we enjoy would never have been constructed. Question everything, even your own beliefs. Anybody can believe whatever they want, and many people just accept the words of others without question.

Ask yourself if you are comfortable with your own beliefs and the beliefs of others. Satisfying your curiosity will help you not only define yourself and your spiritual reality, but it can be a wonderful asset to help you improve your life and the lives of others.

You might ask, "What does this have to do with my spiritual existence? It doesn't sound very spiritual." But it is very spiritual. The ceremonies you experience in the church do nothing for your spiritual self except teach you the laws the preacher wants you to follow. When you exercise your curiosity, you build spiritual muscle. You learn about what helps you and what hurts you. You take steps toward achieving wisdom when you satisfy your curiosities. The little boy admired his wise grandfather. He asked the older man how he could become wise when he was older. The old man told him, "Make lots of mistakes while you are young, son. And learn from them. Make lots of mistakes and learn from them." He is right. People with diminished curiosity lose their chance to grow spiritually. When you satisfy your curiosity, you exercise your spiritual muscle, learn to express yourself, and occasionally learn something beneficial. You are improving your spiritual self.

Imagination

Use your imagination. Your mind is always active, even when you are asleep, in a coma, playing around, or involved in everyday activities. Your vision, which is purely spiritual thought, is primed to become active. Just as with someone's curiosity, people are always willing to downplay their imagination. But just as curiosity helps people discover new ideas and methods of doing things, your imagination will help you enlarge and expand the information your curiosity drives you to discover and explore. Most people have heard "It's just your imagination," as if what you imagine isn't important. Your imagination will lead you to have dreams and discover new ways to create happiness and love in your life. The trick is always to reverse unhappy, losing, or negative thoughts that come up. One easy way to do this is to think of three happy or beneficial ideas every time a depressing thought comes up in your imagination. You imagine when you daydream, sleep, dream, or just let your thoughts wander. Accept it as a very spiritual and natural part of your life. It will open your mind to new, unexplored paths.

Goals

Make goals for yourself. You make goals for yourself continually. Even if you plan to do nothing, it is a goal. Whenever you decide to do anything, start doing it. It is a goal waiting to be accomplished until you do it. It is important to consciously make goals to be in close harmony with your spiritual self. When you willy-nilly float around with no thoughts of your future activities, you lose control of your power to set your destiny. It is imperative to give at least as much credence to your ideas and wishes as to others' thoughts and desires. If you feel your life is a failure, make easy goals for yourself. Achieving your goals, even the small and easy ones, give you good feelings and encourages your spiritual essence to bring new ideas about how to improve your life.

If you put a boat out in the middle of the ocean with no rudder, nothing to power it forward, and no ultimate destination, that boat is going to be at the mercy of whatever waves come along. Having goals, even small ones, gives you the engine to power yourself, a map to follow, and a rudder to steer you. It is easy to plan your life out for a few minutes or a day. There is a saying, "Use it or lose it." Any skill a person has will be lost unless they continue to practice it. Making goals for yourself gives you something to look forward to and keeps you involved in planning for your better future. Even when your dreams are small and easily accomplished, they give you a sense of achievement when completed. Achievement improves your self-esteem and your ability to accept change and adapt to the future. Your efforts also feed your spiritual self and prepare you for an even more delightful future.

Sometime during your life, your energy, both physical and spiritual, will change in such a manner that it is no longer compatible with human acts. Your biological material will slowly change to spiritual energy, and your spiritual energy will rapidly leave your inert physical physique. At that time, you will go back into the spiritual realm. That is what you are working toward right now. We take thoughts and memories with us to our next spiritual existence.

Happiness

Practice happiness. Unhappiness and meanness cripple spiritual growth. Remember that you are a spiritual being walking around with a physical body to help you flourish while on earth. Every thought and everything you do is spiritual. Every moment of your physical life is a spiritual activity. The standard definition of happiness is that it is a state of outstanding well-being and intense emotion. Happiness means the inner state of enjoyable or fulfilling experience as well. Research shows us that unhappy and angry people make many more mistakes and poor decisions than happy people do. Happy people are healthier, enjoy a longer time in human form, and receive more earthly rewards than unhappy people. Smiles, a sign of happiness, attract other people and signal that one is open, nonthreatening, and friendly. When you transcend into the purely spiritual reality, you take your ability to be happy with you. There is a tremendous amount of literature about how to develop the trait of happiness. It is important to study this material because many people claim to be happy but are not happy and do not understand what it is to be happy.

Each of us is responsible for our happiness. We, along with our subconscious, decide whether or not we will be happy. Decide to bring joy into your life and keep it there. When you have a default level of happiness, you will quickly bounce back from trauma and maintain that inner feeling to help you make good decisions about everything you experience.

Respect

Always respect yourself and everyone you encounter. Respect is a feeling of deep admiration for someone or something elicited by their abilities, qualities, or achievements. It is also a high regard for the feelings, wishes, rights, or traditions of others. Sometimes we deal with people we thoroughly dislike or do not want to associate with, but circumstances demand our presence. Dislike and disrespect cloud one's feelings about whomever or whatever they aimed the dislike or disrespect. When you show respect for yourself and whoever you deal with, you accept the value in your own, and their thoughts and actions. It means you treat not only yourself but everyone with high regard, no matter how you feel about their ideas or activities. It requires complete honesty with yourself and anyone with whom you deal. The more you deal with others with honesty, forthrightness, and kindness, the more respect you will have for yourself, and the more likely you will receive respect from them. You will also improve the chances that you will make wise decisions in everything you do.

Honesty

Be honest with yourself and others. Human beings communicate emotionally and verbally. In any conversation, it is easy for one individual to misunderstand what is said to them. It is also easy for the person who did the speaking to allow the incorrect communication to persist. It is easy to emotionally pick up what other people want in any exchange of words. When this happens, it is also easy to tell the other person whatever they want to hear. Always convey the truth to others, even when you know they want something else to be true. Many people, out of their desire to be polite, allow falsehoods to persist. Speak with honesty, accuracy, and sincerity. Do it with empathy and, if possible, with a smile. This will help you build self-respect and focus on your spiritual essence. Most of the time, whoever you speak with will accept your explanations when you correct their understanding of what you meant to convey. They will not only respect your honesty, but will appreciate your integrity and develop a strong trust in everything you say.

Change

Accept and encourage change. Movement and change are omnipresent throughout the universe. Everything changes. It is a universal phenomenon. Learn to expect it and benefit from it. Whenever anything changes in your life, it brings up a possibility for you to learn a lesson about how to experience joy, gratitude, a challenge of some type, or an opportunity to evolve in harmony with the universal spiritual essence and the spiritual essence of your soul. Remember that change is forever. It is up to you to cooperate with change to benefit and raise your spiritual level of wisdom, happiness, and functionality.

Love

Love yourself and others. People often want others to help them feel happy or good. When someone makes them feel better, they believe they love the other person and put themselves under the other person's control. You feel love when you desire to make the other person happy or successful without making demands of loyalty or possession. Love is "I want you to be happy." Dependency is, "I want you to make me happy." Loving yourself means doing whatever you can to improve your health, knowledge, and wisdom. With love, affection is a natural part of earthly living. It is essential to show affection for those you love. We are talking about a happy feeling. When you love, you want what is best for the object of your emotion. There is no jealousy, possessiveness, or resentment involved in true love. The kind of love that will best prepare you for your next existence is a powerful feeling of joy, support, and peace about whomever you direct it. This love has the strength to withstand any confusing behavior of others with whom you may have to deal. It is a beautiful feeling, and those who can carry this feeling with them have an exemplary life while on the earth's plain. They will also be well-prepared to enter their next period of existence.

Gratitude

Practice gratitude. Gratitude is a beautiful feeling of being thankful for what you receive or already have. Many people, given everything they want, may never experience gratitude. The things they own, and stuff provided to them, become expected, and a presumed right. Gratitude is simply being thankful, showing appreciation, or feeling good about words, actions, or deeds. It shows appreciation for the kindness and returns it. It doesn't even have to be kind. Someone can do hurtful things to you that teach you a lesson about them and yourself and life. If you get anything out of it, you can be gracious about it. You can take pleasure in your ability to learn from every experience with honor and dignity.

Gratefulness grows from forming the habit of appreciating everything that comes into your life. You can even enjoy the small stuff. Every day, review five to ten things you are grateful for. These things can be as simple as the sun coming out for a little while or someone smiling at you. You can be thankful that you are alive or are no longer associated with someone who mistreated you. Many people never learn how to have gratitude. They either have a poor attitude about life and everything they experience, or they refuse to believe that anything they receive is an addition to their life.

Do this every day for at least four to six weeks until it becomes habitual. In the beginning, you may feel as if you are merely going through the motions. Still, your spiritual self will respond and rewire you to become grateful for everything. The ability to be grateful will help you grow your self-esteem, self-confidence, and ability to feel and express honest love. Practice feeling gratitude every day until it becomes natural to you. There is a plethora of information about what gratitude is and how to develop the trait. Dare to study it. The idea is to train your spiritual essence regularly to find joy, especially if you want to carry joy with you when your spiritual energy disperses into purely spiritual reality. This is building spiritual muscle, and you can be proud of yourself every time you give thanks for anything.

Environment

Improve your environment. You are a spiritual being existing in a unique, so-called physical world. You can experience incredible happiness, deep love, horrible pain, and extreme suffering. You are responsible for whether you improve your spiritual energy or allow it to become lost or confused. As you affect your environment and those around you, environmental factors of your surroundings also affect you. If you are around people who treat you poorly, it is up to you to convince them to treat you well or abandon them. Many people will justify staying in an unhappy environment, claiming that the other person is occasionally nice to them, or the other person needs them, and the difficulty doesn't bother them. But it does.

A drop of rain falling on a rock does not seem to do any damage. When you put a rock down and allow water to drip on it slowly, the water's continual activity will destroy the stone in a matter of time. The same will happen to you if you sacrifice yourself to put up with someone else's problems. It is lovely when you can help someone who can appreciate it. Those who treat you poorly will never appreciate it unless they somehow decide to. It is also unlikely that they will change their relationship with you unless you tell them to, so they will understand and accept it. When mired in an unsatisfactory relationship, the best thing you can do for yourself and everyone else in the same environment is to leave it. Leaving will allow you to create a better atmosphere for yourself. And your absence from the old domain will leave a void there that has a chance of being improved–or made worse. Whatever happens, it will create change, and whenever there is change, there is a chance for improvement to emerge.

Health

Take care of your health. Healthy people have an advantage over unhealthy people. They are usually more robust, more mobile, and better able to function in every way. To be healthy, you must exercise your body, eat proper foods, and get enough sleep at night so you are well-rested every day. Taking care of your mind is also essential. Sick or disabled people can advance also; they just start at a different level. Doctors constantly claim that a patient with a positive mental attitude heals better and faster than the world's negative Nellies. A disabled person who takes proper care of his or her body will enter their next stage of existence prepared to have excellent health, no matter what their body's makeup is during this present life.

Humility

Be humble. People rarely think about being humble. But when you focus on any people you know who are humble, you will probably see that they are friendly people. A truly humble person is not arrogant and accepts that no one is better or worse than anyone else, since we are all formed from spiritual energy. We are all born with different basic skills, default emotions, hair colors, and various skin colors. But whatever differences we can point out in others, they are all made of the same essential energy. We just use it differently.

It takes effort to escape the role-playing of the often-inharmonious actuality of everyday living. But as you progress on your spiritual path, you will achieve a certain level of success in your worldly endeavors. This can be a real danger if you get so caught up in your success that you neglect your spiritual health. It is necessary to keep an unpretentious attitude about everything you do. There is no need for you to try to impress other people. When you allow your true spiritual self to express itself, there is no need to look down on others. They will readily accept you and probably admire you. There is no need to brag or pretend you are anything different than you are. This is one status all genuinely spiritual people strive for.

Mentors

Find mentors and people to look up to. As spiritual creatures, we not only have a strong sense of curiosity, but we also mimic the actions of people in our environment. When we associate with mean people, we tend to develop similar traits. When we associate with loving friends, we tend to become more loving. During our everyday activities, we meet many individuals exhibiting different types of behavior. When you notice a person who displays qualities you feel are exceptionally good, it is wise to emulate them. Use them as role models or as a mentor. You probably have the same unique qualities. When you imitate them but not copy them, you tend to develop the same qualities they have.

Communication

Develop your communication skills. Listen to understand before you answer—and then speak with clarity. When people engage in conversation, they rarely listen attentively to the person doing the talking. They are thinking about what they want to say next. People converse with others and gain nothing from the conversation because they do not understand what the other person is talking about. Listen to understand, learn, and empathize. Then, with a clear mental understanding of what the other person says, respond with honesty and clarity and in the proper tone of happiness, anger, or whatever you intend to express. Try to be understood.

You are traveling toward a beautiful existence. It is not always an easy or rewarding journey. As you go through your spiritual development, others may try to pull you back to where you were because they were comfortable with your old demeanor. You will possibly intimidate other people, and some may dislike you because they want what you have.

Remember that you are a spirit who temporarily uses a physical body to experience new and ever-changing possibilities during your travels to nirvana. This book has covered many aspects of your spiritual reality, but there are many more for you to learn and explore. It is your choice to make it a dull, hurtful slog or an incredible, exciting adventure. You can meditate, practice gratitude, and express such qualities as love and happiness or whatever you want.

You are alive right now, and this is your life. No matter how good or bad your present situation is, you have the spiritual ability to improve it. Cooperate with your spiritual energy with love and joy. Not only will you improve your life, but you will prepare for your future spiritual journey.

THOUGHTS

- You are a soul using a body
- Your soul feels the same pain and pleasure as your body does
- Your aura is the outermost part of your soul
- Your soul uses your body the best it can
- Your eternity will witness many mistakes and so-called misbehaviors
- There is a solid case to be made for reincarnation
- You are allowed to keep learning throughout eternity
- Spiritual living is like physical living
- You are responsible for your soul

CHAPTER 14

GO FORTH WITH JOY

Have you ever asked yourself what kind of mood you're in? You are always in some kind of mood. It can be good, bad, happy, sad or any way you want to describe it. A mood is a temporary state of mind or feeling. In contrast to emotions or feelings, our moods are less specific, less intense, and less often provoked by a particular stimulus or event. Even though moods are temporary, you are always in a mood. Our moods are important. They are you expressing yourself to yourself and to the world. To get the most out of yourself and the time you spend on earth, it is important for you to be in the proper mood to do it. Our moods are usually relatively stable and often described as positive or negative. They are less intense than emotions but are spiritual messages about how we feel about our existence. Various factors influence them like fatigue, stress, social interactions, world events, hormones, hunger, the weather, and one's general health. Our mood significantly impacts every aspect of our life, including how to feel and behave. These affected states can, in turn, impact our motivational levels, decision making, and our relationship with others.

Early theories about mood focused on its connection to emotion. Recent research has shown physiology and cognition influence our mood. Our mood can play a role in how we learn, remember information, and make decisions. It can also affect our physical health. For example, research has shown that depressed people are more likely to get sick and are more likely to have heart problems than people who aren't depressed. Mood can be difficult to describe, but some common signs will help you decide whether you are in a good mood or a bad mood. They usually define good moods as a positive state of being, although often people can't pinpoint why they are in a good mood. When you feel physically well, free of stress, and are in a positive social relationship, you are probably in a good mood. Common signs of being in a good mood are optimism, happiness, feeling content, feeling energized, and being interested or curious about things.

Common signs of being in a bad mood include anger, feeling sad, anxious, feeling emptiness or hopeless, feeling tired and sluggish, feeling disconnected and disengaged from life, or irritability, or being short-tempered. Negative moods influence how people interpret events and their judgments. Your mood affects everything you do or think. When people are in a more negative mood, they are likely to see events around them in a less than pleasant manner. A range of non-specific factors can influence moods. This makes it more difficult to point to the exact causes of them. Research suggests that poor sleep, environmental factors, stressful negative events, and negative social interactions often occur before developing depressed moods. Researchers discovered that poor sleep quality was associated with mood in one study. They discovered that poor sleep quality was associated with a worse mood. They didn't find that good moods had beneficial effects on sleep quality.

If you are down and out, or feeling a little depressed, there is one little known quick fix that will work for you. At least it works for many people. It is a simple smile. Although factors that influence mood are complex and varied, studies have found that changing your voluntary facial expressions can influence your mood. Smile! Even faking it can often improve your mood. Adopting a positive facial expression will influence your mind and normally bring about a more positive mood, whether or not your smile is genuine. It will also help to take a walk. Studies have found that having contact with nature can have a positive effect on mood and well-being. You can walk out your front door and spend a few minutes looking at the trees, flowers, or whatever is out there, and it will raise your mood. Even if you live in a crowded city, walking outside can help. The change of scenery does it.

Your mood can have a significant impact on your health and well-being. Mood disorders, such as depressive disorders, are associated with an increased risk to your physical health, including heart disease and stroke. One study found that people with a history of depression had a thirty-four percent higher risk of experiencing a stroke. Having a stroke can be a downer big time. Your moods affect the way you function in everyday life. Depressed people have a difficult time making wise decisions, concentrating, and even sleeping. Your moods also influence your relationships with others. People who are depressed or anxious often have trouble communicating and connecting with other people. They are normally reluctant to verbalize exactly how they feel because they don't understand it themselves. This can make it more difficult for them to maintain interpersonal relationships and contributes to feelings of loneliness and social isolation.

Visualize a happy future

Everyone experiences low moods from time to time, but some strategies can help you improve your mood when you are feeling down. Some tips for improving mood include getting regular exercise. Moving your body helps because it will cause you to release millions of endorphins, which are chemicals that have mood-boosting effects. Studies have found that exercise can play a role in improving mood. Besides preventing and easing symptoms of depression, single sessions of exercise offer an immediate chance to improve one's mood. Eating nutritious foods helps improve energy levels and overall well-being, and evidence shows that what you eat can also impact your mood. The link between diet and depression is not fully understood, but there is a growing belief that what you eat provides benefits for boosting mood and fighting depression. Studies have linked the consumption of foods such as highly processed foods high in sugar and fat and red meats to an elevated risk of depressive symptoms.

Simple things like spending time outside, can help to reduce stress and promote relaxation. One study reported that as little as 10 minutes spent sitting or walking outside had a significant positive impact on mood. Also, spending time with loved ones, or taking part in activities with others helps to improve mood and reduce feelings of isolation. Research suggests that positive social interactions help ease depressed moods. When you are under stress, your body produces a chemical called cortisol. It prepares your body to deal with what you are facing, but exposure to too much of it for too long can produce a variety of negative health effects. In fact, studies have shown that cortisol levels are more elevated in people who are more depressed. Relax. It absolutely makes no sense to allow oneself to become overstressed. And it is an unhealthy way to exist. Minimizing stress helps to improve your overall mood. Relaxation techniques, such as yoga, meditation, or deep breathing, help reduce stress and promote feelings of calmness.

Another determiner of your mood is what you expect your life will be like in the future. By future, we are talking about anytime from the coming few seconds all the way to the end of your life. Studies show that having something to look forward to boosts your mood, relaxes you, and relieves your stressful feelings. "Imagining good things ahead of us makes us feel better in the current moment," says Simon A. Rego, chief psychologist at Montefiore Medical Center and Albert Einstein College of Medicine in the Bronx, New York. "It can increase motivation, optimism, and patience and decrease irritability."

Since you spend only a limited time visiting earth during your travels through eternity, spend a few minutes thinking about the place you would like to go to during your next incarnation. Think about the interesting things you will do to prepare for it. Visualize what you plan to look like and see yourself receiving plenty of love and admiration during that time. Thinking about your next life may be a little far off, but you can get excited about a party you want to have for yourself or even a piece of clothing you can buy for yourself. The idea is to practice having an upbeat mood.

Enjoy your life

Many people will belittle or criticize the idea of practicing or rehearsing to be in a good mood, but other people will say it makes a lot more sense to put some effort into having a good mood than to wonder around feeling in the doldrums all the time. Just look around. People successful in their chosen endeavor enjoy their work. They become successful because they enjoy what they need to do, and they will normally put in extra work when they need to. My friend Elvis hires people to work in his manufacturing company. He says that when he hires someone, he tells them to do A, B, and C to get their work done. He said his better employees not only do A, B, and C, they find D, E, and F to do, and they do it. He said they are the ones who get promoted and they often get hired away from him for better paying jobs. They are the ones who use the full power or their spiritual energy and make genuine progress during their stay on earth.

Elvis also told me he feels the reason many people fail at their jobs or chosen vocation is simply because they give up too soon. They take on a project and start out full of excitement or maybe with a poor attitude and the work becomes a little difficult. So, they give up when, if they had stuck with it for a little longer, they would have succeeded. There are a lot of Danny Downers in the world. We all run into them at some time or another and they are always very eager to tell us what won't work, how difficult it is, and there is no use in doing anything. Look. You are alive. You can exist in a state of happiness, or you can be one of those Danny Downers. Life is a lot more interesting and fun if you have some success in your life and choose to enjoy it.

Final Thoughts

- Moods are always with us
- Our moods are relatively stable
- Moods affect our health
- Moods are less intense than emotions
- Moods are spiritual signals about our personal feelings in life
- Moods reflect how we fare in everyday life
- You are responsible for your own moods
- Visualize and affirm to experience good moods
- Become an expression of love and joy
- You have permission to experience happiness
- You are allowed to love anyone you want to love
- Listen to your spiritual essence
- You have the talent and right to be a winner. Be one

ABOUT THE AUTHOR

Walter Broach is a 21st century doctor of Metaphysics and a beacon of knowledge in a realm where few dare to travel. He enlightens and empowers people with his prolific writing skills and unique insights.

His mission is to unravel the complexities of the fundamental energies of the Universe and make them accessible to the world at large. He breaks down the complexities of spiritual energy into understandable language, ensuring that curious minds grasp even the most profound subjects.

Walter Broach is an exceptional writer, known for his ability to distill complex concepts into understandable language. With a profound understanding of spirituality and our interconnectedness with the universe, he has captivated the minds of readers worldwide. His writings offer a unique perspective that resonates with individuals seeking spiritual clarity and enlightenment.

Through his well-balanced and eloquent prose, Broach illuminates the intricacies of the human experience as it relates to spiritual reality, providing insight into our purpose and place in the grand tapestry of existence. His words carry the power to inspire the reader to delve deeper into the mysteries of their own life and embark on new, exciting spiritual journeys.

Beyond his literary accomplishments, Walter Broach leads a fulfilling personal life. He is a loving husband to his wife Ellen and a proud father of six successful children, each forging their paths in different parts of the country. His ability to balance his professional success with strong familial bonds serves as a testament to his character and values.

If you're searching for literature that combines deep, profound spirituality with a down-to-earth approach, Walter Broach's works are a must read. His works are not religious. They are about basic spiritual energy, which is a component of the soul. Dive into his writing and you will discover a treasure trove of wisdom and inspiration that will leave an indelible impact on your heart and mind.

END

www.ingramcontent.com/pod-product-compliance
Lightning Source LLC
Chambersburg PA
CBHW040803120726

48005CB00012B/1285